CARING & COOKING FOR THE HYPER- ACTIVE CHILD

MARY JANE FINSAND

FOREWORD BY JAMES D. HEALY, MD, FAAP

S **Sterling Publishing Co., Inc.   New York**

Oak Tree Press Co., Ltd London & Sydney

OTHER BOOKS OF INTEREST
Allergies and Your Family
Caring and Cooking for the Allergic Child
The Complete Diabetic Cookbook

Library of Congress Cataloging in Publication Data
Finsand, Mary Jane.
  Caring and cooking for the hyperactive child.

  Includes index.
  1. Hyperactive child syndrome—Diet therapy—Recipes.
I. Title. II. Title: Cooking for the hyperactive child.
RJ506.H9F57   641.5′631   80-54335
ISBN 0-8069-5560-0   AACR2
ISBN 0-8069-5561-9 (lib. bdg.)
ISBN 0-8069-8980-7 (pbk.)

Oak Tree ISBN 7061-2795-1

Copyright © 1981 by Mary Jane Finsand
Published by Sterling Publishing Co., Inc.
Two Park Avenue, New York, N.Y. 10016
Distributed in Australia by Oak Tree Press Co., Ltd.
P.O. Box J34, Brickfield Hill, Sydney 2000, N.S.W.
Distributed in the United Kingdom by Oak Tree Press Ltd. U.K.
Available in Canada from Oak Tree Press Ltd.
% Canadian Manda Group, 215 Lakeshore Boulevard East
Toronto, Ontario M5A 3W9
Manufactured in the United States of America

Contents

Foreword

A nutritious, well-balanced diet is a necessity for normal child growth and development. Children (and adults) who eat appropriate amounts and proper kinds of food have fuller, richer, more successful lives. Hyperactive children are no exception. In addition, people who practice good dietary nutritional habits tend to be less susceptible to illness and disease.

Hyperactive children have the same general nutritional needs as the average child. However, Dr. Ben F. Feingold's dietary research and other scientific studies have shown that certain chemicals tend to contribute to hyperactivity. These chemicals are the natural salicylates, artificial colorings, artificial flavorings, BHT (butylated hydroxytoluene), and BHA (butylated hydroxyanisole).

One of the major problems with all controlled or restricted diets is providing a wide variety of tastes, dishes, and meals that are easy to prepare and fun to eat. Mary Jane has combined her expertise as a mother, nutritionist, and cook to create a wide range of tasty recipes that expands the options for hyperactive diet cooking.

Versatility is one of the most important features of any cookbook. The fact that this cookbook includes metric measures (grams, °C, millilitres, etc.), customary measures (ounces, °F, cups, etc.), range/oven cookery, and microwave directions, is most commendable. These multiple features expand the versatility of the book to a broad range of common-sense applications.

In my opinion, this book will be useful to all families who are interested in practicing good dietary nutritional habits. Mary Jane has created an excellent kitchen reference.

—JAMES D. HEALY, M.D., F.A.A.P.

Introduction

Who among us does not like children? Responsive, energetic, well-behaved children are a joy to their parents, friends, and families. However, all children are not like this. Some are not a joy to be around. They can be disruptive, restless, and impulsive. Not only the parents, but the teachers, peers, and entire family are affected by this behavior.

Many of these children are diagnosed as hyperactive. There are many theories on how to treat these children, ranging from drugs affecting the central nervous system to behavior modification and food intake.

In 1973, Dr. Ben F. Feingold introduced a diet which eliminated artificial colors, artificial flavors, BHT (butylated hydroxytoluene), BHA (butylated hydroxyanisole), and fruits and vegetables containing natural salicylates. This diet has had remarkable success in the treatment of the hyperactive child. However, as Dr. Feingold states, the greatest success is when the entire family adheres to the diet.

Although it is always great fun to cook from scratch, I found that time was sometimes a problem when trying to comply completely with this diet. *Caring and Cooking for the Hyperactive Child* is designed to relieve you of some of that time in the kitchen. I have developed quick mixes for cakes, biscuits, puddings, and other convenience foods.

I owe a debt of gratitude to the many mothers, relatives, and friends of hyperactive children who challenged me to prepare certain foods, and who gave generously of recipes, tips, and personal hints. Without their help, this collection of recipes would not be as useful and modern as it is. This cookbook is meant to be used daily for family meals and snacks—I hope you will find it easy and fun to use.

MARY JANE FINSAND

CARING FOR YOUR HYPERACTIVE CHILD

Hyperactivity is one of several labels used to describe a condition in children characterized by impulsive, excessive movement and impaired attention span. This condition is also known as *attention deficit disorder* (ADD), *hyperkinetic syndrome,* and *minimal brain dysfunction* (MBD). According to 1980 estimates, in the United States alone there are nearly 700,000 children suffering from these symptoms, which interfere with the child's ability to perform well both academically and socially. The causes of this disorder are not yet definitely known, and until recent years, therapy consisted primarily of controlling or modifying the symptoms. In 1972, however, Dr. Ben Feingold implicated food additives as the etiological basis for the hyperkinetic syndrome. Modern scientific and technological methods of food preparation and preservation have seen the increasing use of food colorings and flavorings to improve products or to allow for speed in processing and packaging.

In 1973, Dr. Feingold constructed a dietary program for hyperactive children which eliminates artificial colors and flavors and all food containing natural salicylates. The eliminated additives abound in many juvenile diets: in candy, soda, ice cream, bologna, ketchup, etc. Natural salicylates occur in such popular fruits as apples, cherries, and oranges. The influence of diet on hyperactivity remains a topic of continuing controversy. However, up to 50% of the children tested responded positively to the Feingold diet and experienced a decrease in hyperactive symptoms.

The following material in this chapter is extracted from the Association for Children with Learning Disabilities' pamphlet, *Taking the First Step to Solving Learning Problems.*

In 1964, a group of concerned parents formed the ASSO-CIATION FOR CHILDREN WITH LEARNING DISABIL-ITIES. It is the only national organization devoted to defining and finding solutions for the broad spectrum of learning problems. ACLD has 50 state affiliates with more than 785 local chapters. Membership totals over 80,000, including parents, professionals from many sectors, and concerned citizens.

Learning Disabilities occur in many forms . . . visual, auditory, motor control, communication, logic, etc. Effective correction must include a total approach to the educational, physiological, psychological and medical needs of the individual child. Therefore, ACLD believes in an interdisciplinary approach with these major goals:

- ENCOURAGE research in neuro-physiological and psychological aspects of Learning Disabilities.
- STIMULATE development of early detection programs.
- CREATE a climate of public awareness and acceptance.
- DISSEMINATE information widely.
- SERVE as an advocate.
- DEVELOP and PROMOTE legislative assistance.
- IMPROVE regular and special education.
- ESTABLISH career opportunities.

An inquiry to the National ACLD office or to the local ACLD chapter may be a crucial first step in providing help for a person with Learning Disabilities. National Headquarters has a resource library of over 600 publications for sale, in addition to providing a film rental service. Published six times annually, the official ACLD newsletter, NEWS-BRIEFS, covers current developments in the field of Learning Disabilities.

Association for Children with Learning Disabilities
4156 Library Road, Pittsburgh, PA 15234 • 412/341-1515

ACLD is a non-profit organization. Its financial support comes from membership dues, publication sales, conference proceeds, grants and donations. Basically a volunteer effort on all levels, ACLD policies are determined by elected officers and a Board of Directors comprised primarily of parents.

LEARNING DISABILITY—WHAT IS IT?

Each child, adolescent, or adult with a learning disability is unique; each shows a different combination and severity of problems. A learning disability person is an individual who has one or more significant deficits in the essential learning processes.

The learning disability person is usually considered to have near average or above average intelligence. However, for some reason (sometimes known, sometimes not) there is a gap between potential and achievement.

HOW WIDESPREAD IS THE PROBLEM?

Many experts believe that there are between 5,000,000 to 10,000,000 (5 to 10 million) children suffering from some type of learning disability. Percentage of incidence ranges from a conservative 2% estimate (which would include only the most severe cases) to a broad-based 20% of the total school-age population. Recent research indicates that undetected learning disabilities may be the chief problem of a large number of children who do not do well in school. This group would include those children and youths with disciplinary problems and those termed "underachievers" and "dropouts." There is insufficient research to confirm the present number of adults with learning disabilities.

WHY A PERSON HAS A LEARNING DISABILITY

There is no known simple, general explanation why a person has a learning disability. What should be focussed upon is the formulating of a positive plan of action and seeing that plan implemented at school, home, and the community. This plan should include a competent diagnosis, sound educational planning, and treatment of individuals with regard to their strengths and weaknesses.

SYMPTOMS OF LEARNING DISABILITY

The symptoms of learning disabilities are a diverse set of characteristics which affect development and achievement. It is important to note that some of these symptoms can be found in all children at some time during their development. However, *a learning disability person has a cluster of these symptoms* which do not disappear with advancement in age. The most frequently displayed symptoms are: short attention span; poor memory; difficulty following directions; inadequate ability to discriminate between and among letters, numerals, or sounds; poor reading ability; eye-hand coordination problems; difficulties with sequencing; disorganization; and numerous other problems which may affect all of the sensory systems. An expanded list of symptoms is included below:

- performs differently from day to day
- responds inappropriately in many instances
- restless, can't stay interested in anything very long, easily distracted
- says one thing, means another
- difficult to discipline
- doesn't adjust well to change
- immature speech
- doesn't listen well or remember
- can't follow multiple directions
- forgets easily
- has difficulty telling time and telling right from left
- has trouble naming familiar people or things
- has difficulty sounding out words
- writes poorly
- reverses letters or places them in incorrect sequences—for example, "d" for "b" and "gril" for "girl"
- reads poorly if at all
- poorly coordinated
- trouble understanding words or concepts
- late speech development
- late gross or fine motor development
- impulsive

A child is not necessarily learning disabled if he or she exhibits only a few of these symptoms, since most children show some of them at one time or another. However, a child who has a cluster of these problems needs further examination of his/her possible disability.

HYPERACTIVITY—WHAT IS IT?

The term "hyperactive" has become widely used and widely misunderstood. Much controversy surrounds it. The correct medical terminology is "hyperkinetic syndrome." Hyperactivity is often used interchangeably with the term "hyperkinesis." Hyperkinesis describes a condition in which the individual displays a high degree of physical activity which has no purpose, plus a significantly impaired attention span. The person is *unable* to control motion and/or attention. Many physicians have described hyperkinesis as a treatable illness characterized by involuntary behavior and learning problems in a child whose brain maturation is delayed. These physicians feel that the marked tendency of a number of these identified children to improve as they grow older supports this contention.

Cautions

The Health, Education & Welfare report cautioned that the vitality of childhood should not be confused with the very special problems of the child with a hyperkinetic behavior disorder.

Adults who become frustrated with a child's behavior which does not always meet with their standards can easily exaggerate the significance of the child's occasional short attention span or restlessness and label the child hyperactive. Children should be viewed in terms of a developmental sequence: a toddler is more active, restless, and distractible than a school-age child: the younger child is more distractible than the adolescent. *It also must be understood that hyperactivity exists in children with no learning problems.*

Symptoms of Hyperactivity

A hyperkinetic person:

1. fidgets and is restless
2. is inattentive
3. is hard to manage
4. can't sit still
5. is easily distracted
6. has low frustration tolerance
7. is irritable
8. is undisciplined
9. is clumsy
10. is a poor sleeper
11. has emotional lability (quick shift of moods)
12. is socially inept.

Youngsters usually do not suddenly become hyperkinetic. The signals are evident early in the child's life. They are not children who just move a lot because of their age, or nervousness or anxiety stemming from a specific cause.

Diagnosis

Diagnosis of this condition should be conducted by competent professionals: physician, psychologist and/or psychiatrist. This disorder is now more frequently diagnosed than ever before due to the fact that more is known. Nevertheless, some uncertainty still exists. All suspected hyperkinetic children should receive a comprehensive medical and psychological assessment.

LEARNING DISABILITIES PERSONS AND THEIR SOCIAL PERCEPTIONS

Despite the fact that most professionals agree that social adjustment problems are common among many individuals who have learning disabilities, this area has not received much attention. The focus of a learning disability is usually in a learning situation, but the consequences are rarely confined to school or work. Many areas of life are affected, including the role of LD persons in their family, relationships with friends, non-academic functioning such as sports or dancing, and certainly self-image and confidence to handle daily situations.

Some persons with learning disabilities may observe less in their social environment, misperceive more, and may not learn as easily from experience as their friends do. Some children may exhibit an immaturity and social ineptness due to their learning disability. Like many of us, learning disability persons want acceptance, but their eagerness may cause them to try too hard in inappropriate ways.

Behaviors

Common behavior characteristics of learning disability individuals are:

- An inability to read and interpret environment and people
- An inability to adequately interpret their problems and needs
- Little thought about the results of their actions—poor judgment
- Poor impulse control
- A need for immediate gratification
- Inability to set realistic priorities and goals
- Inappropriate conclusions due to deficient reasoning ability
- Illogical reasons for their actions—sometimes even contradicting what was previously stated
- Inability to develop meaningful social relationships with others; usually these children are loners
- Inability to draw appropriate conclusions due to poor reasoning
- Childish and bossy behavior
- An overabundance of frustration, resulting in disruptive behavior.

REHABILITATION ACT OF 1973

"The Civil Rights Act for the Handicapped"

In September, 1973, Congress passed a law that prohibits discrimination on the basis of physical or mental handicaps in every federally assisted program in the country. Sections of this which are of particular importance to the handicapped follow.

Section 504 of this Act stipulates that handicapped people have the following rights:

- As a disabled job applicant or employee, you have the same rights and benefits as a non-handicapped applicant and employee.
- As a disabled person, you are entitled to all medical services and medically-related instruction available to the public.
- As a disabled person, you have the right to participate in vocational rehabilitation, senior citizen activities, day care (for your disability child) or any other social service program receiving federal assistance on an equal basis with non-handicapped.
- You have the same rights as anyone else to go to college or enroll in a job training or adult post-high school basic education program. Your selection must be considered solely on the basis of your academic or other school records. Your disability is not a factor.
- Your state and local school district must provide under Section 504 an appropriate elementary and secondary education for your physically or mentally handicapped child. This public program must cost no more than it costs parents of non-handicapped children.

ADVICE FOR PARENTS

How Can I Find Out if My Child Needs Special Education Services?

Before it can be determined whether or not a person has a learning disability, the following steps should be taken:

1. Schedule a thorough visual, hearing and medical examination to see if the suspected learning disabilities are related to any of these areas. Once the child's visual, hearing and medical condition have been determined, you may need to take the next step which is to:
2. Approach the school district and request a careful assessment of the child's intellectual ability and academic achievement. This testing is done at no cost to the parent.
3. Obtain a written report containing conclusion and recommendations of the evaluation team.

If you believe the school has failed to adequately identify the student as one who requires special services, you may require a due process hearing.

If I Disagree with the Results of the Evaluation, Do I Have Any Other Option?

If you are dissatisfied with the school's evaluation service, you may wish to get an independent evaluation for the student. This should be performed by a competent diagnostic service.

Under some circumstances the school will assume the cost of such an evaluation. If you desire the evaluation, you should write to the school and request that they pay for this service prior to arranging for the testing services. A refusal to pay for the evaluation may be an issue for a due process hearing.

Eligibility for Special Education Services

Once a diagnosis is made and it is felt that the student needs special education services, an individual educational plan is written.

What Is an Individual Education Program (IEP)?

The IEP is a written agreement among all parties, clearly setting forth a statement of what will be provided for the student.

What Must the IEP Contain?

The IEP must include the following:

1. The present levels of performance.
2. The annual and short-term learning goals, i.e., how much the student is expected to learn over a certain period of time.
3. The special education program and related services which will be provided to accomplish these goals.
4. The extent to which the student will participate in regular education programs, i.e., when, where, and how much time he/she will be with non-handicapped students.
5. When special services will begin and how long they will last.
6. When and how the effectiveness of the plan and the student's performance will be evaluated.
7. Evaluate at least annually.

What Other Related Services Are Available to My Child under Public Law 94-142?

Depending upon the student's unique needs, one or more of the following related services should be provided for in the IEP:

- Audiology and Speech
- Psychological Services
- Medical Services for evaluation and diagnostic purposes
- Physical and Occupational Therapy
- Early Identification
- Social Work Services
- Counseling Services
- School Health Services
- Parent Counseling and Training
- Transportation.

The Hyperactive Diet and Your Family

All recipes have been developed to eliminate artificial colors and flavors, BHT, BHA, and the fruits and vegetables which contain natural salicylates (p. 17). A selection from each of the four food groups (p. 16–17) should be eaten at every meal.

Plan each meal to be as unhurried as possible. Dining can relieve tension and anxiety if you sit down to an attractive table. Use color and shapes of food to make it pleasing to the eye as well as appetizing. Remember, a relaxing, interesting meal lends itself to relaxed, interesting conversation and attitudes. An old adage says: "We live by our stomachs." The mood created at mealtime can be the mood we have all day.

THE FOUR FOOD GROUPS

MILK GROUP
Milk: whole, 2%, skim, evaporated, dry, buttermilk
Cheese: pure cheese, cottage cheese, cream cheese
Ice Cream
Children under 10 and adults: 2 or more cups (500 mL) per day
Children over 10 and teenagers: 3 to 4 or more cups (750 to 1000 or more mL) per day

MEAT GROUP
Any meats, poultry, fish, eggs, dry beans, nuts
Two or more 3-oz. (90-g) servings per day

VEGETABLE GROUP

Any fruits or vegetables (except those containing natural salicylates)

Four or more ½-cup (125-mL) servings per day

BREAD AND CEREAL GROUP

Breads, cereals, potatoes, crackers, rice, pasta

Four or more ½-cup (125-mL) servings per day

FRUITS, VEGETABLES, AND OTHER FOODS CONTAINING NATURAL SALICYLATES

Almonds

Apples (including cider and cider vinegar)

Apricots

Berries

Cherries

Cloves

Cucumbers (including cucumber pickles)

Currants

Grapes

Green Peppers

Mint

Nectarines

Oranges

Peaches

Plums

Prunes

Tangerines

Teas

Tomatoes

Oil of Wintergreen

CUSTOMARY TERMS		METRIC SYMBOLS	
t.	teaspoon	mL	millilitre
T.	tablespoon	L	litre
c.	cup	g	gram
pkg.	package	kg	kilogram
pt.	pint	mm	millimetre
qt.	quart	cm	centimetre
oz.	ounce	° C	degrees Celsius
lb.	pound		
°F	degrees Fahrenheit		
in.	inch		

GUIDE TO APPROXIMATE EQUIVALENTS

Customary:				Metric:	
ounces; pounds	cups	tablespoons	teaspoons	millilitres	grams; kilograms
			¼ t.	1 mL	
			½ t.	2 mL	
			1 t.	5 mL	
			2 t.	10 mL	
½ oz.		1 T.	3 t.	15 mL	15 g
1 oz.		2 T.	6 t.	30 mL	30 g
2 oz.	¼ c.	4 T.	12 t.	60 mL	
4 oz.	½ c.	8 T.	24 t.	125 mL	
8 oz.	1 c.	16 T.	48 t.	250 mL	
2.2 lb.					1 kg

Keep in mind that this is not an exact conversion, but generally may be used for food measurement.

GUIDE TO PAN SIZES

Baking Pans

Customary:	Metric:	Holds:
8-in. pie	20-cm pie	600 mL
9-in. pie	23-cm pie	1 L
10-in. pie	25-cm pie	1.3 L
8-in. round	20-cm round	1 L
9-in. round	23-cm round	1.5 L
8-in. square	20-cm square	2 L
9-in. square	23-cm square	2.5 L
9 × 5 × 2-in. loaf	23 × 13 × 5-cm loaf	2 L
9-in. tube	23-cm tube	3 L
10-in. tube	25-cm tube	3 L
10 in. bundt	25-cm bundt	1 L
9 × 5-in.	23 × 13-cm	1.5 L
10 × 6-in.	25 × 16-cm	3.5 L
13 × 9 × 2-in.	33 × 23 × 5-cm	3.5 L
14 × 10-in. cookie tin	35 × 25-cm cookie tin	
15½ × 10½ × 1-in. jelly-roll	39 × 25 × 3-cm jelly-roll	

Cooking Pans and Casseroles

Customary:	Metric:
1 qt.	1 L
2 qt.	2 L
3 qt.	3 L

OVEN COOKING GUIDES

Follow this guide for oven temperature:

Fahrenheit ° F	Oven Heat	Celsius ° C
250–275°	very slow	120–135°
300–325°	slow	150–165°
350–375°	moderate	177–190°
400–425°	hot	200–220°
450–475°	very hot	230–245°
475–500°	hottest	250–290°

Use this meat thermometer probe guide to check the meat's internal temperature:

Fahrenheit ° F	Desired Doneness		Celsius ° C
140°	Beef:	rare	60°
160°	Lamb:	medium	70°
180°	Pork and Veal:	well done	80°
185°	Poultry:	well done	85°

Use this candy thermometer guide to test for doneness:

Fahrenheit ° F	Test		Celsius ° C
230–234°	Syrup:	Thread	100–112°
234–240°	Fondant/Fudge:	Soft Ball	112–115°
244–248°	Caramels:	Firm Ball	118–120°
250–266°	Marshmallows:	Hard Ball	121–130°
270–290°	Taffy:	Soft Crack	132–143°
300–310°	Brittle:	Hard Crack	149–154°

MAKING NATURAL FLAVORINGS

Many flavorings can be obtained by using the seeds, pulp, or milk of plants:

Plant	Plant Part	Flavor
Anise	seed	licorice
Avocado	pulp	avocado
Banana	pulp	banana
Cantaloupe	pulp	cantaloupe
Cranberry	juice or pulp	cranberry
Coconut	pulp or milk	coconut
Frejoa	pulp	strawberry-pineapple
Grapefruit	juice or peel	grapefruit
Guava	juice	guava
Lemon	juice or peel	lemon
Lime	juice or peel	lime
Mango	pulp	peachlike
Papaya	pulp	peachlike
Pear	pulp	pear or apple
Pineapple	juice or pulp	pineapple
Watermelon	juice	watermelon

Nut flavors can be obtained in natural oils or by boiling the nut in a small amount of water, then pulverizing the mixture in a food processor or blender.

MAKING NATURAL FOOD COLORING

Fruits and vegetables can be used to make natural food coloring, without worrying that the flavor of the plant will be tasted: Add a small amount of water to plant. Bring to boil. Simmer over low heat. Strain. Use liquid obtained for coloring. This may be boiled down if you wish a stronger color, and also frozen for future use.

Red Color:
Cranberries
Beets
Red cabbage plus lemon juice

Yellow Color:
Red onion skins
Sunflower petals
Marigold petals
Lemon rind

Green Color:
Fresh spinach
Dandelion, or any edible green leaf

Blue Color:
Red cabbage (be careful this does not
come in contact with a citric acid)

APPETIZERS AND NIBBLES

Chicken Liver and Mushroom Pâté

2 slices	bacon	2 slices
¼ c.	mushroom pieces	60 mL
¼ c.	onion (minced)	60 mL
1 lb.	chicken livers	500 g
½ c.	sweet butter	125 mL
¼ c.	heavy cream	60 mL
½ t.	basil	2 mL
¼ t.	nutmeg	1 mL
¼ t.	marjoram	1 mL
¼ t.	thyme	1 mL
¼ t.	salt	1 mL
dash	pepper	dash
	fresh parsley (minced)	

Fry bacon in skillet until browned and crisp. Remove; add mushrooms, onion, and chicken livers to bacon drippings. Fry over low heat for 10 minutes. Add bacon. Cool slightly; purée in blender or food processor. Melt butter in skillet; add cream and seasonings. Heat thoroughly. Add butter mixture to liver pâté. Blend until creamy. Pour into well-greased mold. Refrigerate 4 hours or overnight. Unmold onto cold serving platter. Sprinkle with minced fresh parsley.

Yield: 3 c. (375 mL)

Mushroom Canapés

½ c.	sweet butter	125 mL
3-oz. pkg.	cream cheese	90-g pkg.
1 c.	all-purpose flour	250 mL
1 t.	salt	5 mL
½ t.	garlic powder	2 mL
½ t.	thyme	2 mL
¼ t.	oregano	1 mL
½ c.	mushroom pieces (chopped fine)	125 mL

Cream together butter and cheese. Blend in remaining ingredients, except mushrooms. Chill thoroughly. Roll out thinly on lightly floured board. Cut with 2-in. (5-cm) cookie cutter. Place ½ t. (2 mL) mushroom pieces in center of each canapé. Fold and seal. Bake at 400° F (200° C) for 10 minutes.

Yield: 15 to 20 servings

Cheese Wafers

1 recipe	pie crust	1 recipe
1 t.	paprika	5 mL
½ t.	garlic powder	2 mL
½ t.	thyme	2 mL
½ c.	Swiss cheese (grated)	125 mL

Prepare pie crust, mixing paprika, garlic powder and thyme into the dough. Chill. Roll out thinly on lightly floured board. Cut into square or round wafers. Place on ungreased cookie sheet. Prick with fork. Bake at 425° F (220° C) for 10 to 12 minutes or until lightly browned. Place mound of cheese in center of wafer. Return to oven for 2 minutes or until cheese melts. Serve hot.

Yield: 20 to 25 servings

Sweet Celery

	celery (rinsed)	
¼ c.	pure peanut butter	60 mL
3-oz. pkg.	cream cheese (softened)	90-g pkg.
¼ c.	walnuts (chopped)	60 mL
2 T.	dates (chopped fine)	30 mL

Cut celery into 2-inch (5 cm) stalks. Cream peanut butter and cheese. Thoroughly stir in walnuts and dates. Fill hollows of celery. Cover lightly and chill.

Yield: ½ c. (125 mL) spread

Pineapple-Glazed Bananas

½ c.	crushed pineapple (with juice)	125 mL
1 t.	lemon juice	5 mL
½ t.	cornstarch	2 mL
4	bananas (peeled)	4
⅓ c.	walnuts (chopped)	90 mL
	whipped cream (optional)	

Combine pineapple, lemon juice, and cornstarch in small saucepan. Cook and stir over low heat until slightly thickened and clear. Place bananas in individual banana boats or dessert dishes. Spoon warm pineapple sauce over bananas. Top with nuts and whipped cream, if desired.

Yield: 4 servings

Tuna Spread

7-oz. can	tuna (drained)	200-g can
2 T.	pure or homemade Mayonnaise (p. 95)	30 mL
1 T.	chives or onion (minced)	15 mL

Combine all ingredients in blender or food processor. Blend until smooth. Pack into bowl; chill thoroughly. Serve with crackers or tortilla chips.

Yield: 1 c. (250 mL)

Ham Spread

1 c.	ham (cooked and diced)	250 mL
1 T.	onion (chopped)	15 mL
1 T.	celery (chopped)	15 mL
2 T.	Mayonnaise (p. 95)	30 mL
2 t.	dry mustard	10 mL

Combine ham, onion, and celery in blender or food processor. Blend until smooth. Stir in Mayonnaise and dry mustard until well blended. Pack into bowl; chill thoroughly. Serve with crackers or tortilla chips.

Yield: 1 c. (250 mL)

Avocado Spread

1	avocado	1
½ c.	summer squash	125 mL
1	onion (chopped fine)	1
1 T.	pure vegetable oil	15 mL
1 T.	lemon juice	15 mL
1 T.	distilled white vinegar	15 mL
1 t.	garlic powder	5 mL
¼ t.	salt	1 mL

Mash avocado and squash with a fork. Add remaining ingredients. Stir to blend.

Yield: 1½ c. (375 mL)

Hikers' Snack

2 c.	dates (cut up)	500 mL
1 c.	pure chocolate chips	250 mL
½ c.	walnut pieces	125 mL
½ c.	coconut (diced small)	125 mL

Combine all ingredients in airtight jar. Shake to mix.

Yield: 3 c. (750 mL)

Cheese-Olive Spread

15	green olives	15
10	black olives	10
8-oz. pkg.	cream cheese (softened)	240-g pkg.
1 t.	milk	5 mL
¼ t.	lemon juice	1 mL

Dry and finely chop green and black olives. Combine cream cheese, milk, and lemon juice. Whip until smooth; add olives. Stir to blend. Serve with crackers.

Yield: ½ c. (125 mL)

Fried Puffs

1 c.	all-purpose flour	250 mL
1 c.	potato (whipped)	250 mL
1	egg (well beaten)	1
1½ t.	baking powder	7 mL
½ t.	salt	2 mL
½ c.	milk	125 mL
	pure vegetable oil	

Combine all ingredients in mixing bowl. Stir well to blend. Drop by heaping tablespoons into hot oil (375° F; 190° C). Fry until golden brown. Serve with cheese spreads or honey.

Yield: 24 to 30 puffs

Bleu Cheese Dip

8-oz. pkg.	cream cheese	220-g pkg.
½ c.	bleu cheese (crumbled)	125 mL
¼ c.	heavy cream	60 mL
1 T.	chives (chopped)	15 mL
1 t.	thyme	5 mL
½ t.	salt	2 mL

Soften cheeses to room temperature. Combine all ingredients and blend well. Serve with pure potato chips or taco chips.

Yield: 1½ c. (375 mL)

Mini Meatballs

1 lb.	beef (ground)	500 g
¼ c.	onion (minced)	60 mL
¼ c.	celery (minced)	60 mL
1	egg (well beaten)	1
½ t.	bay leaf (finely crushed)	2 mL
	salt and pepper to taste	

Combine all ingredients in a mixing bowl. Stir to blend thoroughly. Shape into 50 meatballs. Fry in skillet until brown; roll to turn. Place in shallow dish. Bake at 350° F (175° C) for 20 minutes. Drain. Place on hot serving platter or chafing dish.

Microwave: Cook on High for 4 to 5 minutes. Drain. Place on hot serving platter or chafing dish.

Yield: 50 meatballs

Candied Nuts

1 c.	pecan halves	250 mL
1 c.	walnut halves	250 mL
1 c.	peanuts (unsalted)	250 mL
1	egg white	1
1 T.	water	15 mL
¾ c.	sugar	190 mL
1 T.	cinnamon	15 mL
1 t.	nutmeg	5 mL
½ t.	salt	2 mL

Combine nuts in large mixing bowl. Beat egg white with water until frothy. Pour over nuts. Toss until all nuts are wet. Drain off excess egg white. Add remaining ingredients. Toss to coat completely. Spread on ungreased cookie sheet. Bake at 250° F (120° C) for 25 to 30 minutes. Shake or stir every 10 minutes to prevent sticking.

Yield: 3 c. (750 mL)

Stuffed Olives

Stuff one of the following into well-drained, pitted olives (ripe or green), using pastry tube or tip of spoon:

CHEDDAR CHEESE

1 c.	white Cheddar cheese (grated)	250 mL
2 T.	sweet butter	30 mL
⅓ c.	all-purpose flour	90 mL
1 t.	paprika	5 mL
½ t.	salt	2 mL

Cream together cheese and butter. Blend in flour, paprika, and salt.

ANCHOVY

3-oz. pkg.	cream cheese	87-g pkg.
2-oz. tube	anchovy paste	58-g tube

Whip cheese and anchovy paste until smooth.

HAM AND SWISS CHEESE

2 T.	sweet butter	30 mL
½ c.	white Swiss cheese (grated)	125 mL
½ c.	ham (cooked and grated)	125 mL

Cream together butter and cheese. Stir in ham.

BACON

4 slices	bacon	4 slices
3-oz. pkg.	cream cheese	87-g pkg.
¼ c.	butter	60 mL

Fry bacon until crisp. Cool and crumble into bits. Whip cheese and butter until smooth. Stir in bacon bits.

OTHER STUFFING SUGGESTIONS

Walnut halves	Wiener sticks
Pecan halves	Mushrooms
Water chestnuts	Zucchini
Small whole shrimp	Small cauliflowerettes

Shrimp Island

1 lb.	shrimp	500 g
4	eggs (hard cooked)	4
3 T.	Mayonnaise (p. 95)	45 mL
2 T.	Tomatoless Ketchup (p. 98)	30 mL
1 T.	lemon juice	15 mL
1 T.	parsley (chopped)	15 mL
1 T.	onion (chopped fine)	15 mL
½ t.	salt	2 mL
¼ t.	pepper	1 mL

Cook shrimp. Peel, devein, and place in bowl. Add hard cooked eggs and mash with fork or put through sieve. Add remaining ingredients; mix well. Tightly line a 3-c. (750-mL) bowl with plastic wrap; pack mixture into bowl and cover. Refrigerate 3 to 4 hours or overnight. Unmold onto chilled platter. Remove plastic wrap. Surround shrimp mold with thinly sliced rye bread.

Yield: 2 c. (500 mL)

Coconut Chips

1	coconut	1
	salt	

Crack the coconut by puncturing soft eyes with ice pick or sharp knife. (Drain off liquid into glass or bowl; reserve for other recipes.) Bake coconut at 350° F (175° C) for 30 to 40 minutes. Place on hard surface, eyes up, and hit sharply with hammer. Remove white meat from shell with back of spoon. Peel remaining brown skin off with potato peeler. Slice coconut meat into thin slices or slice in food processor with wide slicer. Place on 14 × 10-in. (35 × 25-cm) cookie tin. Bake at 375° F (190° C) for 20 to 30 minutes or until crisp and lightly browned. Shake or turn every 5 minutes. Salt lightly while hot. Cool.

Yield: 3 c. (375 mL)

Stuffed Mushrooms

1 lb.	whole mushrooms	500 g
2 cloves	garlic	2 cloves
3	green onions	3
¼ c.	sweet butter	60 mL
1 c.	bread crumbs (fine)	250 mL
	mozzarella cheese (shredded)	

Wash mushrooms and remove stems. Finely chop stems, garlic cloves, and green onions. Melt butter in skillet. Add mushroom stem mixture and bread crumbs; sauté. Pack into mushroom caps. Broil for 3 to 4 minutes. Sprinkle with cheese. Place in broiler for a few seconds to melt cheese.

Yield: 10 to 12 servings

Lobster Aspic

¼ c.	water (boiling)	60 mL
1 env.	unflavored gelatin	1 env.
¾ c.	Mayonnaise (p. 95)	190 mL
¼ c.	pure sour cream	60 mL
1 T.	Tomatoless Ketchup (p. 98)	15 mL
2 T.	lemon juice	30 mL
2 t.	distilled white vinegar	10 mL
2 c.	lobster (cooked and diced)	500 mL
10	stuffed green olives (sliced fine)	10
10	pitted black olives (sliced fine)	10
	salt and pepper to taste	

Pour boiling water over gelatin; stir to dissolve. Combine remaining ingredients. Stir well to blend. Add gelatin; thoroughly mix into lobster mixture. Pour into well-rinsed or plastic-wrapped 9-in. (23-cm) loaf pan. Refrigerate until firm.

Yield: 3 c. (750 mL)

SOUPS AND STEWS

Lentil Soup

1 c.	lentils	250 mL
1 qt.	water	1 L
¼ lb.	side (salt) pork (cut up)	250 g
1	onion (chopped)	1
3	carrots (shredded)	3
	salt and pepper to taste	

Combine lentils, water, and side pork in soup kettle. Bring to boil; reduce heat and simmer 3 hours. Add onion and carrots. Season to taste. Cook 1 hour.

Yield: 1 qt. (1 L)

Cream of Avocado Soup

2 c.	Cream of Chicken Soup (p. 34)	500 mL
¼ c.	avocado (puréed)	60 mL
¼ c.	heavy cream	60 mL

Heat Cream of Chicken Soup to boiling. Remove from heat. Add avocado and cream.

Yield: 2½ c. (625 mL)

Chicken Noodle Soup

1 qt.	Chicken Stock (p. 37)	1 L
½ c.	celery (chopped)	125 mL
1½ c.	noodles (cooked)	325 mL
1½ c.	chicken (cooked and diced)	325 mL
	salt and pepper to taste	

Pour Chicken Stock into soup kettle; bring to boil. Reduce heat; add celery. Cook 5 minutes. Add noodles and chicken. Add salt and pepper to taste. Serve hot.

Microwave: Combine Chicken Stock and celery as above. Cook on High for 15 minutes. Add noodles and chicken. Allow to rest 5 minutes. Add salt and pepper to taste. Reheat on Medium for 10 minutes. Serve hot.

Yield: 1½ qt. (1.5 L)

Old-Fashioned Vegetable Soup

2 qt.	Beef Stock (p. 37)	2 L
¼ c.	lima beans	60 mL
1 c.	carrots (diced)	250 mL
½ c.	potatoes (diced)	125 mL
½ c.	celery (chopped)	125 mL
½ c.	peas	125 mL
¼ c.	corn	60 mL
¼ c.	green beans (cut)	60 mL
¼ c.	rutabagas (diced)	60 mL
1 c.	noodles (broken and cooked)	250 mL
¼ c.	cabbage (shredded)	60 mL
¼ c.	onions (chopped)	60 mL
	garlic powder	
	salt and pepper to taste	

Combine Beef Stock and lima beans in soup kettle. Bring to boil; reduce heat and simmer 30 minutes. Add remaining ingredients. Simmer 30 minutes or until vegetables and noodles are tender.

Yield: 2½ qt. (2.5 L)

New England Clam Chowder

3 slices	side (salt) pork (cut up)	3 slices
1 qt.	clams (washed and chopped)	1 L
1	onion (finely chopped)	1
1 qt.	milk (cold)	1 L
2 c.	potatoes (cooked and diced)	500 mL
3 T.	all-purpose flour	45 mL
	salt and pepper to taste	
3 T.	sweet butter	45 mL

Fry side pork over low heat until crisp. Add clams and onion. Sauté for 5 minutes. Pour mixture into soup kettle. Add 3 c. (750 mL) of the milk and the potatoes. Cook over low heat until warm. Combine remaining 1 c. (250 mL) milk and the flour in screwtop jar. Shake well to thoroughly mix. Gradually add to clam mixture. Add salt and pepper to taste. Cook to desired thickness. Add butter. Serve hot with crackers.

Yield: 1½ qt. (1.5 L)

Beef and Barley Soup

2 qt.	Beef Stock (p. 37)	2 L
½ c.	barley	125 mL
½ c.	onions (diced)	125 mL
3	potatoes (cooked and diced)	3
2 c.	beef (cooked and diced)	500 mL
	salt and pepper to taste	

Combine Beef Stock, barley, and onions in soup kettle. Bring to boil; reduce heat. Cook for 1 hour or until barley is tender. Add potatoes and beef. Add salt and pepper to taste. Cook 15 minutes. Serve hot.

Microwave: Combine as above. Cook on High for about 5 minutes and reduce heat to Low. Cook 20 minutes. Add remaining ingredients. Cook 5 minutes. Serve hot.

Yield: 1½ qt. (1.5 L)

Noodles and Ground Beef Soup

1 lb.	beef (ground)	500 g
1 qt.	water	1 L
1 c.	celery (chopped)	250 mL
½ c.	onions (chopped)	125 mL
1 T.	parsley (chopped)	15 mL
1½ c.	noodles (cooked)	325 mL
	salt and pepper to taste	

Combine beef, water, celery, onions, and parsley in soup kettle. Bring to boil; reduce heat and simmer 30 minutes. Add noodles. Add salt and pepper to taste.

Microwave: Combine as above. Cook on High for 5 minutes; reduce heat to Low and cook for 5 minutes. Add noodles. Add salt and pepper to taste.

Yield: 1½ qt. (1.5 L)

Cream of Chicken Soup

2 c.	Chicken Stock (p. 37)	500 mL
½ c.	celery (chopped)	125 mL
¼ c.	onion (chopped)	60 mL
2 c.	milk (cold)	500 mL
2 T.	all-purpose flour	30 mL
2 c.	chicken (cooked and diced)	500 mL
1 T.	sweet butter	15 mL
½ t.	paprika	2 mL
	salt and pepper to taste	

Pour Chicken Stock into soup kettle. Add celery and onion; bring to boil. Reduce heat and simmer 10 minutes. Combine milk and flour in screwtop jar; shake thoroughly to mix. Gradually pour milk into stock. Cook to desired thickness. Stir in chicken, butter, paprika, and salt and pepper to taste. Serve hot or cool to use in casseroles.

Yield: 1 qt. (1 L)

Corn and Cheese Chowder

1	pork chop (bite-size pieces)	1
1 T.	pure vegetable oil	15 mL
½ c.	celery (chopped)	125 mL
¼ c.	onion	60 mL
2 c.	milk (cold)	500 mL
2 c.	corn	500 mL
1 c.	potatoes (cooked and diced)	250 mL
¼ t.	paprika	1 mL
½ t.	thyme	2 mL
2 T.	all-purpose flour	30 mL
1 c.	white Cheddar cheese (shredded)	250 mL
	salt and pepper to taste	

Sauté pork in vegetable oil until brown. Add celery and onion; sauté 5 minutes. Pour into soup kettle. Add 1 c. (250 mL) of the milk, the corn, potatoes, paprika, and thyme. Heat until warm. DO NOT BOIL. Combine remaining 1 c. (250 mL) milk with flour in screwtop jar. Shake until thoroughly blended. Gradually add to corn mixture. Add cheese. Cook over low heat until cheese is melted and soup is desired thickness. Add salt and pepper to taste.

Yield: 3 c. (750 mL)

Beef Vegetable Soup

2 lb.	chuck roast	1 kg
2 qt.	hot water	2 L
1 c.	onions (diced)	250 mL
1 T.	salt	15 mL
2	bay leaves	2
1 c.	carrots (sliced)	250 mL
1 c.	potatoes (diced)	250 mL
½ c.	celery (sliced)	125 mL

Remove meat from bone; cut into small pieces. Add meat and bone to hot water. Bring to boil. Reduce heat and add onions, salt, and bay leaves. Simmer 1 hour. Remove bay leaves. Add remaining ingredients. Simmer 30 minutes. Remove bone before serving.

Yield: 6 to 8 servings

Cream of Celery Soup

2 c.	Chicken Stock (p. 37)	500 mL
1 c.	celery (chopped)	250 mL
2 T.	onion (chopped)	30 mL
1 t.	parsley (chopped)	5 mL
2 c.	milk (cold)	500 mL
2 T.	all-purpose flour	30 mL
2 T.	sweet butter	30 mL
	salt and pepper to taste	

Pour Chicken Stock into soup kettle. Add celery, onion, and parsley; bring to boil. Reduce heat and simmer 10 minutes. Combine milk and flour in screwtop jar; shake thoroughly to mix. Gradually pour milk into stock. Cook to desired thickness. Stir in butter, and salt and pepper to taste. Serve hot or cool to use in casseroles.

Yield: 1 qt. (1 L)

Clam Chowder

2 dozen	clams	2 dozen
2 t.	salt	10 mL
½ t.	pepper	2 mL
1	bay leaf	1
2 qt.	water	2 L
1 c.	celery (diced)	250 mL
½ c.	carrots (diced)	125 mL
½ c.	onions (diced)	125 mL
2 c.	potatoes (diced)	500 mL
¼ c.	all-purpose flour	60 mL
½ c.	water	125 mL
3 T.	sweet butter	45 mL

Add clams, salt, pepper, and bay leaf to the water. Cook until clams open up. Strain off broth into soup kettle. Chop clams. Add celery, carrots, onions, and potatoes to clam broth; simmer until vegetables are tender. Combine flour and water in screwtop jar. Gradually add to soup to thicken. Add clams and butter. Serve very hot.

Yield: 6 to 8 servings

Beef Stock

4 lb.	chuck roast	2 kg
2 T.	shortening	30 mL
2	onions (sliced)	2
½ c.	celery (sliced)	125 mL
1 t.	thyme	5 mL
3	bay leaves	3
2 t.	salt	10 mL
½ t.	pepper	2 mL
4 qt.	water	4 L

Preheat oven to 450° F (230° C). Remove meat from bone and cut into bite-size pieces. Bone should be left in pot while mixture is cooking. Place shortening in roasting pan and melt in oven. Shake to coat bottom of pan. Add meat and roast uncovered for 20 minutes; stir frequently. Add onions and celery. Roast for 10 minutes more, stirring to keep from burning. Remove from oven and pour meat and vegetables into large soup pot. Add a little water to roasting pan and scrape up all the browned bits. Add to soup pot. Add remaining ingredients to soup; bring to boil. Reduce heat, cover, and simmer 2 to 3 hours. Remove bone from pot. Strain and cool.

Yield: 4 qt. (4 L)

Chicken Stock

3 lb.	chicken (cut up)	1.5 kg
1	onion (sliced)	1
1 c.	carrots (sliced)	250 mL
½ c.	celery with leaves (sliced)	125 mL
½ t.	thyme	2 mL
½ t.	rosemary	2 mL
2 t.	salt	10 mL
½ t.	pepper	2 mL
2 qt.	water	2 L

Place ingredients in large soup pot. Bring to boil; reduce heat, cover, and simmer 2 to 3 hours. Strain and cool. (Remove chicken meat from bones and use for salads or other dishes.)

Yield: 2 qt. (2 L)

Chicken Gumbo Soup

½ c.	celery (diced)	125 mL
½ c.	onions (diced)	125 mL
1 t.	salt	5 mL
½ t.	pepper	2 mL
1 t.	sugar	5 mL
2 T.	sweet butter	30 mL
½ c.	okra (cooked)	125 mL
1 c.	rice (cooked)	250 mL
1 qt.	Chicken Stock (p. 37)	1 L

Season celery and onions with salt, pepper, and sugar. Fry in butter until tender. Add okra, rice, and Chicken Stock. Simmer 15 to 20 minutes.

Yield: 6 to 8 servings

Cream of Vichyssoise

6	leeks, cut in 1-in. (2.5-cm) pieces	6
3 c.	potatoes (sliced)	750 mL
1 qt.	water	1 L
2 c.	chicken (cooked and diced)	500 mL
3 T.	sweet butter	45 mL
1 c.	light cream	250 mL
1 c.	milk	250 mL
1 t.	salt	5 mL
½ t.	pepper	2 mL
2 t.	chives (chopped)	10 mL
dash	paprika	dash

Cook leek pieces and sliced potatoes in the water in a covered pot until tender, about 30 minutes. Remove from water and cool slightly. Process in blender or press through a sieve to cream. Place in saucepan, along with chicken, butter, light cream, milk, salt, and pepper. Stir well. Heat over low heat until hot. Garnish with chives and paprika. Serve hot or icy cold.

Yield: 6 servings

Cream of Mushroom Soup

¼ c.	sweet butter	60 mL
¼ c.	onion (chopped)	60 mL
½ c.	mushroom pieces	125 mL
1 T.	all-purpose flour	15 mL
2 c.	Chicken Stock (p. 37)	500 mL
½ c.	milk	125 mL
	salt and pepper to taste	

Melt butter in soup pot. Add onion and mushrooms. Cook until tender. Blend flour with part of the Chicken Stock in screwtop jar until smooth. Add to remaining stock; stir to blend. Pour into soup pot; heat soup, stirring frequently, until it reaches boiling point. Remove from heat. Stir in milk, and salt and pepper to taste. Reheat before serving.

Yield: 4 to 5 servings

German Spring Soup

1 qt.	Beef Stock (p. 37)	1 L
1	cauliflower (broken in pieces)	1
1 c.	fresh peas	250 mL
2	carrots (sliced)	2
1 c.	green beans (sliced)	250 mL
4	asparagus spears (cut up)	4
1 t.	parsley (chopped)	5 mL
	salt and pepper to taste	

Pour Beef Stock into soup kettle. Bring to boil; reduce heat. Add remaining ingredients. Cover and simmer gently over low heat for 30 minutes or until vegetables are tender.

Microwave: Combine as above. Cook on Low for 15 to 20 minutes

Yield: 1 qt. (1 L)

Country Stew

2 T.	pure vegetable oil	30 mL
1½ lb.	pork shoulder (cubed)	750 g
1½ lb.	beef roast (cubed)	750 g
1 c.	potatoes (cubed)	250 mL
½ c.	carrots (cubed)	125 mL
½ c.	celery (sliced)	125 mL
1	onion (chopped)	1
1 clove	garlic (minced)	1 clove
1½ c.	soup stock	325 mL
2 c.	water	500 mL
1 T.	salt	15 mL
1 T.	parsley (chopped)	15 mL
1 t.	pepper	5 mL
¼ c.	all-purpose flour	60 mL

Heat oil in large skillet or soup kettle. Brown meat over medium heat. Add potatoes, carrots, celery, onion, garlic, soup stock, 1½ c. (325 mL) of the water, salt, parsley, and pepper. Cover. Bring to boil; reduce heat and simmer 1½ hours or until meat is tender. Combine flour and the remaining ½ c. (125 mL) water in screwtop jar. Shake to blend. Slowly stir into meat mixture. Cook to desired thickness.

Yield: 6 to 7 servings

Seafood Stew

2 c.	Cream of Mushroom Soup (p. 39)	500 mL
1 c.	white fish fillet (cut up)	250 mL
½ c.	shrimp (cooked)	125 mL
½ c.	clams (cooked)	125 mL
½ c.	mushroom pieces	125 mL
½ c.	celery (chopped)	125 mL
¼ c.	onion (chopped)	60 mL
2 T.	sweet buter	30 mL
2 T.	sour cream	30 mL
1 T.	lemon juice	15 mL
	salt and white pepper to taste	

Heat Cream of Mushroom Soup in soup kettle until warm. Add fish;

simmer 10 minutes. Add shrimp, clams, mushrooms, celery, and onion. Simmer 10 minutes. Remove from heat. Stir in butter, sour cream, and lemon juice. Add salt and pepper to taste. Serve over biscuits or toast tips.

Yield: 5 to 6 servings

Stew Italiano

2 lb.	beef stew meat	1 kg
2 T.	pure vegetable oil	30 mL
1 qt.	water	1 L
2	onions (quartered)	2
4	carrots (cut into chunks)	4
2 stalks	celery (cut into chunks)	2 stalks
1 lb.	mushrooms (cleaned)	500 g
2 cloves	garlic	2 cloves
½ t.	oregano	2 mL
½ t.	thyme	2 mL
¼ t.	paprika	1 mL
1 T.	salt	15 mL
¼ c.	water	60 mL
2 T.	cornstarch	30 mL
1 c.	sour cream	250 mL

Fry stew meat in vegetable oil until brown. Add 1 qt. (1 L) water, onions, carrots, and celery. Cover and bring to boil; reduce heat and simmer 30 minutes. Add mushrooms, garlic, oregano, thyme, paprika, and salt. Simmer 10 minutes. Combine ¼ c. (60 mL) water and cornstarch in screwtop jar. Shake until thoroughly blended. Add to stew. Cook until clear and slightly thickened. Remove from heat. Stir in sour cream.

Yield: 1½ qt. (1.5 L)

MEAT AND POULTRY

Sauerbraten

3 lb.	beef arm roast	1.5 kg
1 T.	salt	15 mL
½ t.	pepper	2 mL
3 c.	water	750 mL
1 c.	distilled white vinegar	250 mL
½ c.	lemon juice	125 mL
2	onions (quartered)	2
1	carrot (cut in chunks)	1
1 stalk	celery with leaves	1 stalk
2	bay leaves	2
½ t.	ginger	2 mL
½ t.	cinnamon	2 mL
½ t.	nutmeg	2 mL
½ c.	sweet butter	125 mL
1 T.	sugar	15 mL
⅓ c.	all-purpose flour	90 mL
½ c.	water	125 mL

Salt and pepper the roast. Place in large baking pan. Combine 3 c. (750 mL) water, the vinegar, lemon juice, onions, carrot, celery, bay leaves, ginger, cinnamon, and nutmeg in blender or food processor. Blend until liquid. Pour over roast. Marinate 3 to 4 days, turning occasionally. Melt butter in large skillet. Brown roast on both sides. Add marinade liquid; bring to boil. Reduce heat and simmer 3 hours. Combine sugar, flour, and ½ c. (125 mL) water in screwtop jar. Pour into marinade liquid; stir to blend. Cover and continue cooking 1 hour or until meat is tender. Transfer meat to serving platter. Pour some gravy over meat and serve remaining gravy in separate bowl.

Yield: 6 to 8 servings

Matchless Meatballs

1	egg (slightly beaten)	1
2 T.	water	30 mL
1½ c.	bread crumbs (fresh)	325 mL
1 lb.	ground beef	500 g
¼ lb.	ground pork	125 g
¼ c.	onion (minced)	60 mL
1 t.	salt	5 mL
	flour	
½ c.	Beef Stock (p. 37)	125 mL

Combine egg, water, and bread crumbs in bowl. Toss to blend. Add beef, pork, onion and salt to bread-crumb mixture. Beat until smooth. Form into balls; roll in flour. Brown over medium heat; drain off excess fat. Add Beef Stock. Cover; simmer 30 minutes.

Yield: 5 to 6 servings

Pork with Eggplant

½ c.	pure vegetable oil	125 mL
2 large	eggplants, cut into ½-in. (12-mm) cubes	2 large
2 lb.	pork (ground)	1 kg
1 c.	onions (chopped)	250 mL
¼ c.	parsley (chopped)	60 mL
1 t.	salt	5 mL
½ t.	garlic powder	2 mL
⅓ c.	bread crumbs	90 mL
2 T.	sweet butter	30 mL

Heat oil over medium heat. Add eggplant and sauté until tender. Remove. Add pork, onions, and 2 T. (30 mL) of the parsley to skillet. Cook until pork is brown. Drain. Combine pork mixture, eggplant, salt, and garlic powder. Spoon evenly into 6 individual serving dishes or ramekins. Sprinkle with bread crumbs and butter. Bake at 350° F (175° C) for 20 to 25 minutes or until crumbs are brown. Garnish with remaining parsley.

Yield: 6 servings

Stuffed Beef Heart

2 lb.	beef heart	1 kg
1 c.	cracker crumbs (fine)	250 mL
½ c.	thick White Sauce (p. 90)	125 mL
1 c.	chestnuts (roasted)	250 mL
	salt and pepper to taste	
	bread crumbs	

Wash and clean heart. Combine cracker crumbs, White Sauce, chestnuts, salt and pepper to taste. Stir to blend. Fill heart cavity. Pin or sew opening of the heart. Place in large covered skillet or pan. Cover with water; bring to boil. Boil 10 minutes; reduce heat and simmer until tender—about 1 hour. Transfer from skillet into baking dish. Sprinkle with salt, pepper, and bread crumbs. Bake at 350° F (175° C) for 15 to 20 minutes or until brown.

Yield: 5 to 6 servings

Pork Chops with Sage Dressing

¼ c.	sweet butter	60 mL
½ c.	celery (chopped fine)	125 mL
½ c.	onion (chopped fine)	125 mL
2 c.	bread crumbs (dry)	500 mL
2 t.	sage	10 mL
½ t.	salt	2 mL
dash	pepper	dash
3 to 4 T.	water or soup stock	45 to 60 mL
6	rib pork chops with pockets	6

Melt butter in skillet. Add celery and onion. Sauté until onion is tender. Reduce heat. Add bread crumbs, sage, salt, and pepper. Toss to coat with butter. Sauté for 2 to 3 minutes. Remove from heat. Add water or soup stock. Toss to mix. Stuff pockets in chops loosely with stuffing. Fasten pockets securely with toothpicks. Place in baking dish. Cover and bake at 350° F (175° C) for 45 to 60 minutes or until tender.

Yield: 6 servings

Pork Pie

Pie Dough:

2 c.	all-purpose flour	500 mL
⅔ c.	sweet butter	160 mL
½ t.	salt	2 mL
6 to 7 T.	water (cold)	90 to 105 mL

Filling:

1 lb.	pork (cubed)	500 g
1 c.	onions (chopped)	250 mL
1 c.	celery with leaves (chopped)	250 mL
1 clove	garlic (chopped)	1 clove
½ t.	salt	2 mL
¼ t.	cinnamon	1 mL
¼ t.	nutmeg	1 mL
1 c.	water	250 mL
1 c.	bread crumbs (dry)	250 mL

Combine flour, butter, and salt in bowl. Using pastry cutter, cut into pieces until it resembles cornmeal. Add 6 to 7 T. (90 to 105 mL) cold water. Blend into dough. Divide in half; chill.

Combine pork, onions, celery, garlic, salt, cinnamon, nutmeg and 1 c. (250 mL) water in saucepan. Bring to boil; reduce heat and simmer 20 to 25 minutes or until pork is tender. Remove from heat. Stir in bread crumbs. Cover and cool.

Roll half of pie dough to fit the bottom of 9-in. (23-cm) pie pan. Fill with pork mixture. Roll second half to cover pork. Fit and seal tightly. Cut air vents in top crust. Bake at 400° F (200° C) for 30 to 35 minutes.

Yield: 5 to 6 servings

Veal Jambalaya

¼ c.	pure vegetable oil	60 mL
1 lb.	veal (cubed)	500 g
⅓ c.	onion (minced)	90 mL
½ c.	celery (sliced)	125 mL
1 c.	rice (uncooked)	250 mL
1½ c.	water	325 mL
1	bay leaf	1
¼ c.	parsley (chopped)	60 mL
1 t.	salt	5 mL
¼ t.	pepper	1 mL
¼ t.	thyme	1 mL

Heat oil in skillet. Add veal and brown; remove from skillet. Add onion, celery, and rice to skillet. Sauté until onions are tender (about 5 minutes). Stir in the browned veal. Add remaining ingredients. Stir to blend. Reduce heat and simmer until rice is done and liquid is absorbed.

Yield: 5 to 6 servings

Ham, Yams, and Pineapple

1 lb.	ham slice	500 g
1 lb.	yams (cooked, peeled, sliced)	500 g
1 20-oz. can	pineapple slices with juice	1 560-g can
2 T.	brown sugar	30 mL
1 T.	sweet butter	15 mL

Brown ham slice in large skillet. Cover with yam slices and pineapple slices with juice. Sprinkle with brown sugar and dot with butter. Cover and cook over medium heat until all are heated through. Baste several times.

Microwave: Place ham slice in 8-in. (20-cm) square dish. Cover with yam slices and pineapple slices with juice. Sprinkle with brown sugar and dot with butter. Cover. Cook on High for 10 to 12 minutes. Spoon juices over ham and serve.

Yield: 2 to 3 servings

Porcupine Meatballs

¾ c.	milk	190 mL
½ c.	rice (uncooked)	125 mL
1 lb.	ground meat	500 g
1	small onion (chopped)	1
1 t.	baking powder	5 mL
	salt and pepper to taste	

Combine milk and rice in saucepan; bring to boil. Simmer until milk is absorbed. Add meat, onion, baking powder, salt and pepper to taste. Mix thoroughly. Roll into small balls. Place in baking dish; cover. Bake at 350° F (175° C) for 20 to 30 minutes.

Microwave: Cook on Medium for 10 to 12 minutes. Allow to rest 3 minutes before serving.

Yield: 4 servings

Turkey Frankfurters

1 T.	salt	15 mL
1 T.	sugar	15 mL
¼ c.	water (hot)	60 mL
1 lb.	turkey (ground fine)	500 g
¼ lb.	pork (ground)	125 g
1 t.	sage	5 mL
¼ t.	nutmeg	1 mL

Dissolve salt and sugar in water. Combine remaining ingredients. Add sugar water. Mix thoroughly by kneading. Stuff into casings or roll tightly into desired lengths. Cook in water or over low heat on charcoal grill.

Yield: 8 to 10 frankfurters

Chicken Croquettes

2 c.	chicken (cooked and chopped)	500 mL
1 c.	milk	250 mL
3 T.	sweet butter	45 mL
3 T.	all-purpose flour	45 mL
2 t.	salt	10 mL
½ t.	onion juice	2 mL
1 c.	bread crumbs (fine)	250 mL
1	egg (beaten)	1
	pure vegetable oil	

Prepare chicken. Combine milk, butter, flour, salt, and onion juice in saucepan. Cook and stir until thick. Add chicken. Cool completely. Shape as desired. Roll in bread crumbs and chill. Just before frying, roll in beaten egg, and again in bread crumbs. Fry in hot oil (375° F; 190° C) until golden brown.

Yield: 5 to 6 servings

Pork Chops and Rice

1 T.	shortening	15 mL
6	pork chops	6
1 c.	rice (uncooked)	125 mL
1	onion (sliced)	1
2 c.	Beef Stock (p. 37)	500 mL
6	carrots (halved)	6
	salt and pepper to taste	

Melt shortening in skillet. Brown chops over medium heat. Place in single layer in baking dish. Brown rice and onion in same skillet; add Beef Stock. Cover and simmer over low heat until most of liquid is absorbed. Place carrot halves on top of pork chops. Add salt and pepper to taste. Pour rice mixture over meat. Cover and bake at 350° F (175° C) for 1 hour.

Microwave: Cook on Medium for 15 to 20 minutes. Allow to rest 5 minutes before serving.

Yield: 6 servings

Kranska* Sausage

1 lb.	pork (ground)	500 g
1 lb.	beef (ground)	500 g
1 T.	salt	15 mL
½ t.	garlic powder	2 mL
½ t.	thyme	2 mL
½ t.	paprika	2 mL
¼ t.	pepper	1 mL

Combine all ingredients. Mix thoroughly. Stuff into casings or form into patties. Cook in medium-hot skillet or over medium heat on charcoal grill.

Yield: 8 sausages or patties

Quick Oven Chicken

1 c.	cornmeal	250 mL
½ c.	all-purpose flour	125 mL
1 t.	salt	5 mL
½ t.	pepper	2 mL
3 lb.	chicken (cut up)	1.5 kg
½ c.	sweet butter (melted)	125 mL

Blend cornmeal, flour, salt, and pepper. Dip each piece of chicken in melted butter, then roll in cornmeal mixture. Place in single layer on 14 × 10-in. (35 × 25-cm) cookie sheet. Bake at 350° F (175° C) for 1 hour or until golden brown.

Yield: 4 to 5 servings

* Kranska Sausage is named for Mr. Kranska, who makes this tasty dish in Sheboygan, Wisconsin.

Lamb Pilaf

3 T.	sweet butter	45 mL
2 lb.	lamb, cut in 1-in. (2.5-cm) cubes	1 kg
1 large	onion (sliced and ringed)	1 large
½ t.	cinnamon	2 mL
½ t.	pepper	2 mL
2 c.	rice (uncooked)	500 mL
1 c.	dates (chopped)	250 mL
2 t.	salt	10 mL
1 c.	Beef Stock (p. 37)	250 mL
2 c.	water	500 mL
¼ c.	lemon juice	60 mL
¼ c.	pecans	60 mL
1 c.	parsley (chopped)	250 mL

Melt butter in large skillet. Add lamb cubes and sauté until brown. Remove lamb. Add onion rings, cinnamon, and pepper to skillet. Sauté until onions are tender. Layer half of rice, dates, lamb, and onions into well-greased 3-qt. (3-L) casserole. Repeat layers. Sprinkle with salt. Mix Beef Stock and water. Pour over lamb mixture. Cover. Bake at 400° F (200° C) for 1 hour. Remove cover. Sprinkle with lemon juice and pecans. Bake 10 minutes. Garnish with parsley.

Yield: 5 to 7 servings

Bratwurst Sausage

2 lb.	pork (ground)	1 kg
½ lb.	beef (ground)	250 g
1 T.	salt	15 mL
1 t.	sage	5 mL
1 t.	paprika	5 mL
¼ t.	pepper	1 mL

Combine all ingredients. Mix thoroughly. Stuff into casings or form into patties. Cook in medium-hot skillet or over medium heat on charcoal grill.

Yield: 8 to 10 sausages or patties

Summer Sausage

2 lb.	beef (ground)	1 kg
1 lb.	pork (ground)	500 g
2 T.	sugar	30 mL
1 T.	mustard seeds	15 mL
1 t.	sage	5 mL
¼ t.	pepper	1 mL
¼ t.	garlic powder (optional)	1 mL

Combine all ingredients. Mix thoroughly by kneading. Spread meat on cookie sheet or waxed paper. Allow to rest 2 to 3 days in a cool place. Roll into log, 15 to 20 in. (40 to 60 cm) long. Wrap log in washed cheesecloth or muslin, or stuff meat into casings. Allow to age at least a week and dry slightly before slicing.

Yield: 1 log

Spicy Wieners

1 lb.	pork (ground)	500 g
1 lb.	beef (ground)	500 g
½ c.	bread crumbs (fine)	125 mL
1 T.	sugar	15 mL
1 t.	mace	5 mL
½ t.	paprika	2 mL
¼ t.	garlic powder	1 mL

Combine all ingredients. Mix thoroughly by kneading. Stuff into casings or roll tightly into desired lengths. (Wieners may be smoked.) Cook in water or over low heat on charcoal grill.

Yield: 12 to 20 wieners

FISH AND SEAFOOD

Codfish Pudding

2 lb.	cod (skinned and boned)	1 kg
¼ c.	all-purpose flour	60 mL
3 T.	bread crumbs (dry)	45 mL
2 T.	sweet butter	30 mL
2 t.	salt	10 mL
¼ t.	pepper	1 mL
1 c.	light cream	250 mL
1½ c.	heavy cream	325 mL

Combine cod, flour, bread crumbs, butter, salt, and pepper in food processor or blender; blend to purée. (This may be done with rotary beater.) Spoon mixture into large mixing bowl. Combine creams in measuring pitcher. Stir to blend. Slowly beat creams into cod mixture. Beat slowly until mixture is thick. Spoon into well-greased 5 to 6-c. (1250 to 1500-mL) mold or baking dish. Smooth top surface of mixture; cover. Place mold or baking dish in larger pan. Pour boiling water two-thirds of the way up the mold or dish. Bake at 400° F (200° C) for 1 to 1½ hours, or until toothpick inserted in center comes out clean. Unmold or cut into squares to serve.

Yield: 6 to 8 servings

Shrimp 'n' Sauce

Shrimp:

1 lb.	shrimp	500 g
2 T.	sweet butter	30 mL
1	carrot (chopped)	1
1	onion (chopped)	1
1 stalk	celery (chopped)	1 stalk
1 qt.	water	1 L
1 clove	garlic (chopped)	1 clove
2 T.	parsley (chopped)	30 mL
1	bay leaf	1
½ t.	salt	2 mL
¼ t.	thyme	1 mL

Sauce:

2 T.	sweet butter	30 mL
2 T.	flour	30 mL
2	egg yolks	2
1 c.	heavy cream	250 mL

Shell and devein shrimp. Melt 2 T. (30 m̂L) butter in large saucepan. Add and sauté carrot, onion, and celery until onion is tender. Add water and seasonings. Bring to boil. Reduce heat. Place shrimp in wire basket; add to onion broth. Simmer 5 minutes or until shrimp are pink. Remove shrimp and rinse with cold water. Refrigerate. Continue to boil broth until liquid is reduced to 3 c. (750 mL). Keep hot but not boiling.

Combine 2 T. (30 mL) butter and the flour in skillet. Cook and stir until golden brown. Slowly add ½ c. (125 mL) of shrimp liquid. Stir into a smooth paste. Pour into the remaining shrimp liquid in saucepan. Stir to blend. Beat egg yolks in bowl until frothy. Stir in heavy cream. Add small amount of hot shrimp liquid to egg yolks. Slowly add egg yolks to hot shrimp liquid. Cook and stir over low heat until thickened. Remove from heat. Fold in shrimp. Serve over rice, toast, or pastry.

Yield: 4 to 5 servings

Sole Florentine

2 lb.	spinach (cooked and drained)	1 kg
2 lb.	sole fillet	1 kg
2 c.	water	500 mL
1	bay leaf	1
1 T.	lemon juice	15 mL
1 t.	salt	5 mL
½ t.	pepper	2 mL
1 c.	White Sauce (p.90)	250 mL
½ c.	Swiss cheese (shredded)	125 mL

Spread spinach into bottom of well-greased 13 × 9-in. (33 × 23-cm) baking dish. Place sole fillet in large skillet. Add water, bay leaf, and lemon juice. Bring to boil; reduce heat and simmer 5 minutes or until fish flakes. Carefully remove from skillet with slotted spatula. Place sole on top of spinach. Sprinkle with salt and pepper. Heat White Sauce with cheese until cheese melts. Pour sauce over fish. Bake at 400° F (200° C) for 20 to 25 minutes.

Microwave: Cook on High for 10 to 12 minutes.

Yield: 4 to 5 servings

Salmon Spaghettini

1 lb.	salmon (cooked and flaked)	500 g
¼ c.	pure vegetable oil	60 mL
2 T.	parsley (chopped)	30 mL
1 clove	garlic (minced)	1 clove
1	onion (chopped)	1
1 t.	salt	5 mL
¼ t.	white pepper	1 mL
2 lb.	spaghettini or broken spaghetti (cooked)	1 kg

Prepare salmon. Heat oil over medium heat in large skillet. Add parsley, garlic, and onion. Sauté until onion is tender. Add salmon, salt, and pepper. Toss and heat just until hot. Pour over cooked spaghettini. Serve with Parmesan cheese.

Yield: 6 to 7 servings

Steamed Halibut

2 lb.	halibut steaks	1 kg
1	onion (sliced)	1
2	bay leaves (crushed)	2
1 T.	lemon juice	15 mL
½ c.	sweet butter (melted)	125 mL

Place halibut steaks in steamer or cooling rack on 14 × 10-in. (35 × 25-cm) cookie tin; add 2 c. (500 mL) water to cookie line. Cover with onion slices and bay leaves. Sprinkle with lemon juice. Cover tightly. Bake at 350° F (175° C) for 45 minutes. To serve, place halibut steaks on heated serving plate; pour melted butter over steaks.

Microwave: Cook on High for 10 to 12 minutes. Allow to rest for 5 minutes before serving with melted butter.

Yield: 6 servings

Baked Red Snapper

2 lb.	red snapper fillets	1 kg
2 t.	lemon rind (grated)	10 mL
2 t.	grapefruit rind (grated)	10 mL
	salt and pepper to taste	

Put fillets in buttered baking dish. Sprinkle with lemon rind, grapefruit rind, salt and pepper to taste. Cover and bake at 400° F (200° C) for 30 to 40 minutes.

Microwave: Cook on High for 10 to 12 minutes. Allow to rest 5 minutes.

Yield: 6 to 7 servings

Crazy Seafood Pizza

Crust:

1 c.	all-purpose flour	250 mL
2	eggs	2
⅔ c.	milk	160 mL
1 t.	salt	5 mL
1 t.	oregano	5 mL
½ t.	garlic powder	2 mL

Topping:

1 lb.	seafood (chopped)	500 g
2 c.	mushroom pieces	500 mL
1 c.	mozzarella cheese (shredded)	250 mL
1 c.	white Cheddar cheese (shredded)	250 mL

Combine all ingredients for crust. Beat until smooth. Pour into well-greased 15 × 10-in. (39 × 25-cm) jelly-roll pan. Arrange seafood and mushrooms over batter. Bake at 400° F (200° C) for 25 to 30 minutes or until golden brown. Remove from oven; sprinkle with cheeses. Return to oven for 10 minutes or until cheese melts.

Yield: One 15 × 10-in. (39 × 25-cm) pizza

Batter-Fried Shrimp

	pure vegetable oil	
1 c.	Convenience Mix (p. 101)	250 mL
⅓ c.	milk	90 mL
2 lb.	shrimp (shelled and deveined)	1 kg
1 c.	all-purpose flour	250 mL

Heat pure vegetable oil to 375° F (190° C). Combine Convenience Mix and milk. Stir to blend. Dredge shrimp in flour. Dip into prepared mix. Fry shrimp, a few at a time, in deep fat until golden brown. Drain.

Yield: 8 servings

Tuna Roll

1 recipe	Convenience Mix (p. 101)	1 recipe
2 c.	tuna (well drained)	500 mL
½ c.	celery (chopped fine)	125 mL
1 T.	onion (chopped fine)	15 mL
¼ c.	pure or homemade Mayonnaise (p. 95)	60 mL
1	egg white (beaten)	1

Roll biscuit dough out ¼ in. (8 mm) thick on lightly floured board. Combine tuna, celery, onion and Mayonnaise. Stir to blend thoroughly. Spread evenly on biscuit dough. Roll up, jelly-roll style. Seal ends. Place on greased 13 × 9-in. (33 × 25-cm) cookie sheet. Cut slits in top. Brush with beaten egg white. Bake at 400° F (200° C) for 20 to 25 minutes or until golden brown.

Yield: 5 to 6 servings

Baked Fish Dish

3 T.	all-purpose flour	45 mL
2 c.	milk	500 mL
¼ c.	sweet butter	60 mL
1 T.	pure solid shortening	15 mL
½ c.	light cream	125 mL
2 c.	fish (finely flaked)	500 mL
½ t.	salt	2 mL
4	eggs	4
½ c.	bread crumbs (dry)	125 mL

Combine flour and part of milk in screwtop jar. Shake to blend. Heat butter, shortening, remaining milk, and cream in saucepan. Add flour-milk mixture. Heat and stir until smooth and thickened. Stir in fish and salt. Remove from heat. Beat eggs until lemon-colored and foamy. Fold in fish mixture. Spoon into well-greased 9-in. (23-cm) baking dish. Sprinkle with bread crumbs. Bake at 375° F (190° C) for 45 to 60 minutes or until set and lightly browned.

Yield: 6 servings

Salmon Mold

1 lb.	salmon (cooked and flaked)	500 g
2 pkg.	unflavored gelatin	2 pkg.
½ c.	water (cold)	125 mL
½ c.	lemon juice	125 mL
1 t.	salt	5 mL
¼ t.	paprika	1 mL
2 c.	whipped heavy cream	500 mL

Prepare salmon. Soften gelatin in cold water. Stir and cook over low heat until gelatin is dissolved. Remove from heat. Add lemon juice, salt, and paprika. Refrigerate until slightly thickened. Fold in salmon and whipped cream. Spoon into mold. Chill thoroughly. Unmold and garnish with fresh parsley.

Yield: 4 servings

Herbed Shrimp

2 lb.	shrimp	1 kg
½ c.	sweet butter	125 mL
½ lb.	mushrooms	250 g
1 c.	celery (sliced)	250 mL
2 t.	chives (chopped)	30 mL
1 t.	parsley (chopped)	5 mL
1 t.	dry mustard	5 mL
½ t.	tarragon	2 mL
½ t.	thyme	2 mL
½ t.	salt	2 mL
¼ t.	garlic powder	1 mL
dash	pepper	dash
¼ c.	lemon juice	60 mL

Shell and devein shrimp. Melt butter over medium heat in skillet. Add mushrooms and celery. Sauté for 2 minutes. Add shrimp. Mix seasonings together and sprinkle over shrimp. Sauté lightly. Add lemon juice. Cover and simmer 5 minutes. Serve with noodles or rice.

Yield: 4 to 5 servings

Spaghetti with Clam Sauce

½ c.	sweet butter	125 mL
½ c.	pure vegetable oil	125 mL
1 t.	oregano	5 mL
1 t.	garlic powder	5 mL
1 t.	rosemary	5 mL
1 6-oz. can	clams with juice	1 170-g can
½ c.	clam juice	125 mL
1 4-oz. can	mushroom pieces	1 113-g can
	salt and pepper to taste	
1 lb.	spaghetti (cooked)	500 g
	Parmesan cheese	

Melt butter in saucepan. Add oil, oregano, garlic, rosemary, clams with juice, clam juice, mushrooms, salt and pepper to taste. Simmer over low heat for 30 minutes. Pour over cooked spaghetti; sprinkle with cheese.

Yield: 6 servings

Easy Salmon Patties

1 lb.	salmon (cooked and flaked)	500 g
3 slices	bread	3 slices
¼ c.	milk	60 mL
1	egg	1
1 t.	salt	5 mL
¼ t.	garlic powder	1 mL

Prepare salmon. Soak bread in milk. Stir to mash. Add salmon and remaining ingredients. Blend well. Drop by spoonfuls onto hot greased skillet. Flatten slightly with back of spoon. Fry until golden brown. Turn and fry on second side.

Yield: 4 to 6 servings

Tuna Burgers

3-oz. pkg.	cream cheese (softened)	90-g pkg.
1 c.	tuna (drained)	250 mL
½ c.	Swiss cheese (grated)	125 mL
1 t.	salt	5 mL
¼ t.	pepper	1 mL
8	hamburger buns	8

Whip cream cheese until fluffy. Fold in tuna, cheese, salt, and pepper. Spread mixture onto buns. Wrap in aluminum foil. Bake at 250° F (120° C) for 20 minutes or until hot.

Microwave: Combine as above. Wrap in plastic wrap or waxed paper. Cook on Low for 3 to 4 minutes or until hot.

Yield: 8 sandwiches

Shrimp Corn Casserole

2 T.	sweet butter	30 mL
½ c.	onion (chopped)	125 mL
½ c.	celery (chopped)	125 mL
1 lb.	shrimp	500 g
1 t.	salt	5 mL
½ c.	dates (chopped fine)	125 mL
2 c.	corn (cooked)	500 mL
½ c.	milk	125 mL
2 T.	all-purpose flour	30 mL

Melt butter over medium heat in skillet; add onion and celery. Sauté for 3 minutes. Add shrimp, salt, and dates. Reduce heat; cover and cook 2 minutes. Remove from heat. Pour into lightly greased 1½-qt. (1.5-L) casserole. Add corn. Combine milk and flour in screwtop jar. Shake to blend thoroughly. Pour over corn mixture. Fold to mix ingredients. Cover and bake at 350° F (175° C) for 25 to 30 minutes or until set.

Microwave: Combine as above. Cook on High for 12 to 15 minutes or until set.

Yield: 5 to 6 servings

Clam Pilaf

1 c.	clams (cooked and minced)	250 mL
1	onion (finely chopped)	1
⅓ c.	pure vegetable oil	90 mL
1 t.	salt	5 mL
1 c.	rice (uncooked)	250 mL
2 c.	water or broth	500 mL

Prepare clams. In saucepan, sauté onions in hot oil until transparent. Add clams and remaining ingredients. Bring to boil. Reduce heat; stir, cover and simmer until rice is cooked.

Yield: 4 to 5 servings

Norwegian Fish Casserole

3 lb.	whitefish	1.5 kg
1 T.	salt	15 mL
4 c.	potatoes (mashed)	1 L
1 c.	onions (chopped)	250 mL
½ c.	bread crumbs	125 mL
½ c.	heavy cream	125 mL

Place fish and salt in large kettle. Cover with water. Bring to boil; reduce heat and simmer for 30 minutes or until fish flakes. Drain. Cool slightly and remove all good meat. Layer 1⅓ c. (340 mL) potatoes, ½ c. (125 mL) onions, ¼ c. (60 mL) bread crumbs, and half of flaked fish into well-greased 9-in. (23-cm)-square baking dish. Repeat layering, ending with mashed potatoes. Pour cream over entire casserole. Bake at 350° F (175° C) for 1 hour or until lightly browned.

Yield: 5 to 6 servings

Creamed Crab

¼ c.	sweet butter	60 mL
¼ c.	all-purpose flour	60 mL
2 c.	whole milk	500 mL
1 T.	lime juice	15 mL
2 c.	crab meat, picked over	500 mL

Melt butter in saucepan. Add flour and stir until well blended. Slowly add milk, stirring constantly until smooth. Add lime juice. Cook over low heat for 3 to 4 minutes. Add crab meat. Cook until heated through. Serve over rice, toast, or noodles.

Yield: 3 c. (750 mL)

CHEESE AND EGGS

Cheese Summer Rice

4 c.	rice (cooked and cooled)	1 L
½ c.	celery (chopped)	125 mL
¼ c.	carrot (chopped)	60 mL
¼ c.	green olives (sliced)	60 mL
¼ c.	ripe olives (sliced)	60 mL
1 T.	onion (chopped fine)	15 mL
½ c.	pure vegetable oil	125 mL
2 T.	distilled white vinegar	30 mL
1 T.	lemon juice	15 mL
1 t.	salt	5 mL
¼ t.	pepper	1 mL
¼ t.	sugar	1 mL
¼ t.	dry mustard	1 mL
1 c.	white Cheddar cheese (cubed)	250 mL
1 c.	Swiss cheese (julienne strips)	250 mL
1 c.	mozzarella cheese (shredded)	250 mL
	lettuce	
3	eggs (hard-cooked and quartered)	3

Combine rice, celery, carrot, olives, and onion in large bowl. Thoroughly blend together the oil, vinegar, lemon juice, salt, pepper, sugar, and dry mustard. Pour over rice mixture. Toss to mix well. Cover and refrigerate to thoroughly chill. Just before serving, add cheeses. Spoon into lettuce-lined bowl. Garnish with egg quarters.

Yield: 8 to 10 servings

Chinese Scramble

1 c.	onions (chopped)	250 mL
½ c.	celery (sliced)	125 mL
2 T.	sweet butter	30 mL
½ c.	water chestnuts (sliced)	125 mL
¼ c.	bamboo shoots	60 mL
¼ c.	mushroom pieces	60 mL
4	eggs (slightly beaten)	4
1 t.	salt	5 mL
½ t.	pepper	2 mL
1 c.	white Cheddar cheese (shredded)	250 mL

Sauté onions and celery in butter until tender. Add water chestnuts, bamboo shoots, mushrooms, eggs, salt, and pepper. Cook and stir until slightly thickened. Add cheese; cook until cheese is melted. Spoon over chow mein noodles or rice.

Yield: 5 to 6 servings

Savory Egg

1 T.	sweet butter	15 mL
2 T.	onion (finely chopped)	30 mL
2 T.	celery (finely chopped)	30 mL
½ c.	zucchini (grated)	125 mL
1½ c.	white Cheddar cheese (grated)	375 mL
	salt and pepper to taste	
2 T.	milk	30 mL
1	egg	1
4 slices	toast	4 slices

Melt butter in skillet; heat to bubbling. Add onion and celery; cook until soft. Add zucchini. Cook and stir over low heat 5 minutes. Add cheese, salt and pepper to taste. Cook, stirring constantly, until cheese melts. Beat milk and egg together. Stir into cheese mixture; cook until set. Spoon over toast.

Yield: 4 servings

Cheese Quiche Lorraine

9 in.	pie shell (baked)	23 cm
1 T.	sweet butter	15 mL
½ c.	green onions (sliced)	125 mL
½ c.	Swiss cheese (shredded)	125 mL
½ c.	white Cheddar cheese (shredded)	125 mL
4	eggs (beaten)	4
1 c.	milk	250 mL
1 c.	heavy cream	250 mL
1 t.	salt	5 mL
½ t.	white pepper	2 mL
dash	paprika	dash

Prepare pie shell. Melt butter in small skillet. Add green onions and sauté until tender. Sprinkle onion-butter mixture and cheeses over bottom of baked pie shell. Combine remaining ingredients. Stir to blend. Pour into shell. Bake at 450° F (230° C) for 15 minutes; reduce heat to 350° F (175° C) and bake 15 to 20 minutes, or until knife inserted in center comes out clean. Allow to rest 5 minutes before serving.

Yield: One 9-in. (23-cm) pie

Mock Welsh Rarebit

½ c.	soup stock	125 mL
1 t.	dry mustard	5 mL
½ t.	salt	2 mL
dash	paprika	dash
4 c.	white Cheddar cheese (shredded)	1 L
	hot toast, biscuits, or muffins	

Combine soup stock, dry mustard, salt, and paprika in large saucepan. Cook over medium heat until steaming. Reduce heat. Add cheese; cook and stir until cheese is melted. Spoon over hot toast, biscuits, or muffins.

Yield: 4 to 6 servings

Cheese Torte

6	eggs (separated)	6
2 lb.	white Cheddar cheese (grated)	1 kg
3 c.	eggplant (cooked and chopped)	750 mL
3 cloves	garlic (chopped fine)	3 cloves
½ c.	parsley (chopped)	125 mL
	salt and pepper to taste	
	additional grated cheese	

Combine egg yolks, cheese, eggplant, garlic, parsley, salt, and pepper in bowl. Stir to blend. Whip egg whites until stiff. Fold cheese mixture into egg whites. Spread evenly into 13 × 9-in. (33 × 23-cm) baking dish. Sprinkle with additional cheese. Bake at 325° F (165° C) for 1½ hours or until set.

Yield: 6 to 8 servings

Eggplant Parmigiana

1 large	eggplant, sliced ½ in. (12 mm) thick	1 large
2 t.	salt	10 mL
½ c.	olive or pure vegetable oil	125 mL
1	onion (chopped)	1
1 clove	garlic (minced)	1 clove
2 c.	beef soup stock	500 mL
½ t.	basil	2 mL
½ t.	oregano	2 mL
¼ t.	pepper	1 mL
2	eggs	2
3 T.	all-purpose flour	45 mL
¾ c.	Parmesan cheese (grated)	190 mL
1 c.	mozzarella cheese (shredded)	250 mL

Sprinkle eggplant slices with 1 t. (5 mL) of the salt. Allow to rest 30 minutes. Pat dry. Heat oil in saucepan. Add onion and garlic; sauté for 3 to 4 minutes. Add soup stock, basil, oregano, the remaining 1 t. (5 mL) salt, and pepper. Cover; simmer 20 minutes. Combine eggs and flour in small bowl. Beat until smooth. Dip eggplant in egg mixture; drain slightly. Place in single layer in shallow baking dish. Top with half of the soup stock, half of the Parmesan cheese and half of the mozzarella cheese. Repeat layers. Bake at 350° F (175° C) for 25 to 30 minutes.

Microwave: Combine as above. Cook on High for 10 to 12 minutes.

Yield: 6 to 8 servings

Danish Egg Lunch

6 slices	side (salt) pork	6 slices
½ c.	onion (chopped)	125 mL
⅓ c.	celery (chopped)	90 mL
1 c.	Cream of Chicken Soup (p. 34)	250 mL
8	eggs (slightly beaten)	8
6 slices	toast	6 slices

Fry side pork until crisp; remove and crumble. Pour off excess fat, leaving about 2 to 3 T. (30 to 45 mL) in pan. Add and sauté onion and celery until tender. Combine Cream of Chicken Soup and eggs; stir to blend. Pour into pan. Stir and cook over low heat until eggs are set. Spoon onto toast. Sprinkle with pork crumbs.

Yield: 6 open-face sandwiches

Baked Eggs

4	eggs (beaten)	4
2 c.	milk	500 mL
1 c.	homemade Saltine Cracker crumbs (p. 102)	250 mL
½ c.	sweet butter (melted)	125 mL
	salt and pepper to taste	

Combine all ingredients. Pour into greased 9-in. (23-cm) square pan. Bake at 350° F (175° C) for 40 to 45 minutes or until set.

Microwave: Cook covered on Low for 20 to 25 minutes or until set. Stir occasionally. Allow to rest 5 minutes.

Yield: 4 servings

Cheese and Egg Brunch Bake

2 c.	Convenience Mix (p. 101)	500 mL
½ c.	water	125 mL
1 T.	sweet butter	15 mL
1 small	onion (chopped)	1 small
½ c.	mushrooms (sliced)	125 mL
2 c.	Swiss cheese (shredded)	500 mL
4	eggs	4
¼ c.	milk	60 mL
1 t.	salt	5 mL
¼ t.	pepper	1 mL

Combine Convenience Mix and water to make soft dough. Pat into bottom and sides of lightly greased 13 × 9-in. (33 × 23-cm) baking dish. Melt butter in small skillet. Add onion and mushrooms; sauté until onion is tender. Spread onion mixture evenly over dough on bottom of dish. Sprinkle with cheese. Combine eggs, milk, salt, and pepper; beat to blend. Pour over cheese. Bake at 350° F (175° C) for 30 minutes or until knife inserted in center comes out clean.

Yield: 6 to 7 servings

Fettucini alla Papalina

½ c.	sweet butter	125 mL
2 c.	mushrooms (sliced)	500 mL
½ c.	onions	125 mL
4	egg yolks	4
¼ c.	Parmesan cheese (grated)	60 mL
1 qt.	noodles (cooked)	1 L

Melt 2 T. (30 mL) of the butter in small skillet. Add mushrooms and onions and sauté until tender; reserve. Beat egg yolks in top of double boiler. Stir in cheese. Cut remaining 6 T. (90 mL) butter into egg yolks. Place egg mixture over hot (not boiling) water. Cook and stir until butter melts and sauce thickens slightly. Pour egg mixture over hot noodles. Toss to blend. Top with reserved mushroom-onion mixture. Garnish with extra cheese and parsley.

Yield: 4 to 6 servings

Spaghetti with Eggs

½ lb.	spaghetti (cooked)	250 g
¼ c.	sweet butter	60 mL
1	onion (chopped)	1
½ c.	mushroom pieces	125 mL
4	eggs	4
¼ c.	milk	60 mL
1 t.	salt	5 mL
½ t.	pepper	2 mL

Prepare spaghetti. Meanwhile, melt butter in large skillet over medium heat. Add onion and mushrooms; sauté for 5 minutes. Add cooked and drained spaghetti. Toss to blend. Combine eggs, milk, salt, and pepper in bowl; beat to blend. Pour egg mixture over spaghetti. Cook and toss until eggs are set.

Yield: 4 to 5 servings

Cheese Strata

8 slices	bread (slightly dry)	8 slices
2 c.	white Cheddar cheese (grated)	500 mL
4	eggs (beaten)	4
2½ c.	milk	625 mL
1 T.	onion (minced)	15 mL
½ t.	salt	1 mL
¼ t.	dry mustard	1 mL
dash	pepper	dash

Trim crusts from bread. Place 4 slices bread in bottom of well-greased 9-in. (23-cm) baking dish. Sprinkle with half the cheese. Combine remaining ingredients. Stir to blend. Pour half of egg-milk mixture over cheese. Repeat layers. If desired, top with extra cheese. Allow to rest at room temperature for 1 hour or place in refrigerator overnight. Bake at 325° F (165° C) for 1 hour or until toothpick in center comes out clean.

Yield: 6 to 7 servings

Cheese-Stuffed Cabbage Rolls

1 small	cabbage	1 small
2 c.	Swiss cheese (grated)	500 mL
1 c.	potatoes (mashed)	250 mL
2 T.	all-purpose flour	30 mL
2	eggs	2
1 t.	salt	5 mL
½ t.	pepper	2 mL
1 c.	mushrooms (sliced)	250 mL
1½ c.	Chicken Stock (p. 37)	325 mL
1	onion (chopped)	1
1 T.	sweet butter	15 mL

Wash cabbage. Cook in boiling salted water until tender. Drain and rinse with cold water until cool. Combine cheese, potatoes, flour, eggs, salt, and pepper in mixing bowl. Beat until smooth. Stir in mushrooms. Carefully remove leaves from cabbage, one by one. Place 2 T. (30 mL) filling into center of a cabbage leaf. Roll up. Repeat until filling is used. Place in 13 × 9-in. (33 × 23-cm) baking dish. Combine Chicken Stock, onion, and butter in saucepan. Heat to melt butter. Pour over cabbage rolls. Bake at 350° F (175° C) for 45 minutes.

Microwave: Combine as above. Cook on High for 20 minutes.

Yield: 6 servings

VEGETABLES

French-Fried Vegetables

5–6 c. (1250–1500 mL) eggplant, zucchini, cauliflower, broccoli, and onions, all cut or broken into 2½-in. (5- to 6-cm) pieces or strips

	flour	
2	eggs	2
1 c.	milk	250 mL
1 c.	bread crumbs (fine)	250 mL
1 t.	onion salt	5 mL
1 t.	salt	5 mL
½ t.	thyme	3 mL
½ t.	pepper	3 mL
	pure vegetable oil	

Dust vegetables lightly with flour; shake off excess and set aside. Beat eggs and milk until completely mixed. Combine bread crumbs, onion salt, salt, thyme, and pepper in shaker bag. Dip floured vegetables in egg mixture. Place in shaker bag and shake slightly to coat; shake off excess crumbs. Place vegetables in single layer on baking sheet. Chill overnight. Fry in hot oil (375° F; 190° C), until golden brown. Drain. Serve immediately.

Yield: 5–6 c. (1250–1500 mL)

Mushroom Cauliflower

1 medium	cauliflower	1 medium
2 c.	milk	500 mL
¼ c.	all-purpose flour	60 mL
¼ c.	sweet butter	60 mL
1 t.	salt	5 mL
1½ c.	mushroom pieces	325 mL
	paprika	

Separate cauliflower into medium-size pieces. Cook, covered in salted water, until tender (about 10 minutes). Drain. Combine milk, flour, butter, and salt in saucepan. Cook and stir over low heat until thick. Add mushrooms. Remove from heat. Place half of cauliflower on bottom of greased 8-in. (20-cm) square baking dish. Cover with half the sauce. Repeat layers. Sprinkle with paprika. Bake at 350° F (175° C) for 15 minutes.

Yield: 6 to 8 servings

Party Peas

2 c.	peas (fresh or frozen)	500 mL
4	green onions (chopped)	4
1 t.	sugar	5 mL
½ t.	salt	2 mL
¼ t.	thyme	1 mL
dash each	rosemary and pepper	dash each
1 t.	sweet butter	5 mL
½ c.	water	125 mL

Combine all ingredients in heavy saucepan. Cover and cook over low heat until peas are done. Drain. Pour into heated serving dish.

Microwave: Combine as above (except no water). Cover. Cook on High for 4 to 5 minutes.

Yield: 4 to 5 servings

Pear-Acorn Squash

2	acorn squash	2
½ c.	water	125 mL
2 c.	pears (sliced)	500 mL
¼ c.	sugar	60 mL
1 t.	cinnamon	5 mL
¼ t.	salt	1 mL

Cut squash in half lengthwise; remove seeds. Place squash cut-side down in shallow baking dish. Add water. Cover tightly. Bake at 350° F (175° C) for 5 minutes. Uncover. Turn squash over. Fill evenly with pear slices. Sprinkle with sugar, cinnamon, and salt. Cover tightly and return to oven. Bake for 30 to 35 minutes or until squash is tender.

Yield: 4 servings

Honey Baked Beans

2 c.	navy beans (dried)	500 mL
1 t.	baking soda	5 mL
4 slices	side (salt) pork	4 slices
2 c.	water (boiling)	500 mL
¼ c.	honey	60 mL
2 T.	distilled white vinegar	30 mL
1 T.	celery (chopped fine)	15 mL
1 t.	salt	5 mL
½ t.	dry mustard	2 mL
¼ t.	cinnamon	1 mL

Place beans in large saucepan. Cover with water and soak overnight. Drain. Again, cover with water; add baking soda. Bring to boil; reduce heat and simmer until skins start to break—about 3½ hours. Drain. Line baking dish with side pork. Pour in beans. Mix boiling water, honey, vinegar, celery, salt, dry mustard, and cinnamon. Pour over beans. Bake at 350° F (175° C) for 3 to 4 hours or until beans are tender. Add extra water if needed.

Yield: 8 to 10 servings

Greek Zucchini

1 large	zucchini, cut in ¼-in. (6-mm) pieces	1 large
¼ c.	pure vegetable oil	60 mL
¼ c.	lemon juice	60 mL
1	bay leaf	1
2 T.	parsley (chopped)	30 mL
1 t.	salt	5 mL
1 t.	coriander seeds	5 mL
1 t.	garlic powder	5 mL
¼ t.	thyme	1 mL
¼ t.	pepper	1 mL

Combine all ingredients in saucepan. Bring to boil. Reduce heat; simmer for 8 minutes or until zucchini is tender. Transfer zucchini slices to heated dish. Sprinkle with extra parsley.

Microwave: Combine as above. Cook on High for 4 to 5 minutes or until zucchini is tender. Continue as above.

Yield: 4 to 5 servings

Potato Pancakes

1 c.	potatoes (mashed and cooled)	250 mL
2 T.	all-purpose flour	30 mL
½ t.	salt	2 mL
¼ t.	pepper	1 mL
2	eggs	2
¼ c.	heavy cream	60 mL

Combine potatoes, flour, salt, and pepper. Thoroughly beat in eggs, one at a time. Stir in cream. Spoon 3 T. (45 mL) potato batter into warm, lightly greased, 7-in. (18-cm) skillet. Tilt skillet to spread batter evenly. Fry to delicate brown. Flip; brown second side. Turn out onto heated platter. Keep hot in 250° F (120° C) oven while frying remaining batter.

Yield: 10 to 12 pancakes

Cheese Lima Loaf

2 c.	lima beans (cooked)	500 mL
1 c.	bread crumbs (fine)	250 mL
½ c.	white Cheddar cheese	125 mL
2 T.	sweet butter (melted)	30 mL
1 T.	onion (minced)	15 mL
1 t.	salt	5 mL
½ t.	pepper	2 mL

Mash beans. Add remaining ingredients. Stir to completely blend. Place in well-greased loaf pan. Bake at 350° F (175° C) for 45 to 50 minutes or until brown. Turn out onto heated serving dish. Garnish with chopped parsley.

Yield: 6 to 7 servings

Stuffed Eggplant

1 medium	eggplant	1 medium
1 T.	shortening	15 mL
1 lb.	beef (ground)	500 g
1 small	onion (chopped)	1 small
½ c.	mushroom pieces	125 mL
½ t.	sweet basil	3 mL
	salt and pepper to taste	

Wash eggplant. Cut in half lengthwise. Carefully scoop out pulp and dice; reserve eggplant shell. Melt shortening in frying pan. Add beef and onion; fry over medium heat until brown. Add mushrooms, diced eggplant, sweet basil, salt and pepper to taste. Cook, stirring frequently, for 5 minutes. Drain. Spoon meat mixture into reserved eggplant shells. Place shells in shallow baking pan. Add ½ in. (1.25 cm) of water to pan. Bake at 350° F (175° C) for 30 minutes.

Microwave: Cook on Medium 15 minutes. DO NOT ADD WATER TO BAKING DISH.

Yield: 6 to 8 servings

Creamed Carrots and Dates

2 c	carrots (sliced)	500 mL
1½ c.	water	325 mL
2 T.	sweet butter	30 mL
1 T.	flour	15 mL
1 t.	salt	5 mL
1 t.	sugar	5 mL
½ c.	dates (cut up)	125 mL
½ c.	heavy cream	125 mL

Combine carrots, water, butter, flour, salt, and sugar in saucepan. Cover. Bring to boil; reduce heat and simmer 15 minutes. Add dates. Stir to blend. Simmer 5 minutes. Drain any excess liquid. Stir in cream. Cook 1 minute.

Microwave: Combine as above. Cook on High for 4 minutes. Add dates. Stir to blend. Cook on High for 2 minutes. Drain. Stir in cream. Cover. Allow to rest 2 to 3 minutes.

Yield: 4 to 5 servings

Polka Dot Vegetables

1 c.	peas	250 mL
1 c.	corn	250 mL
½ c.	cauliflower	125 mL
¼ c.	water	60 mL
2 T.	sweet butter	30 mL
	salt and pepper to taste	

Combine vegetables and water in saucepan. Cover. Bring to boil; reduce heat and simmer 7 to 10 minutes or until vegetables are tender. Drain. Add sweet butter, salt and pepper to taste. Heat until butter is melted. Pour into heated serving dish.

Microwave: Combine vegetables in glass bowl (no water). Cover. Cook on High for 4 minutes. Add butter, salt, and pepper. Cook on High 1 minute.

Yield: 5 to 6 servings

Corn Fritters

2 c.	corn (cooked)	500 mL
2	eggs (separated)	2
1 c.	milk	250 mL
1 c.	all-purpose flour	250 mL
1½ t.	baking powder	7 mL
	salt and pepper to taste	
	pure vegetable oil	

Combine corn, egg yolks, milk, flour, baking powder, salt and pepper to taste. Stir to blend thoroughly. Beat egg whites until stiff. Fold corn mixture into egg whites. Drop by spoonfuls into deep hot vegetable oil (375° F; 190° C). Fry until golden brown.

Yield: 6 to 8 servings

Golden Carrot Dish

1 c.	milk	250 mL
2 T.	all-purpose flour	30 mL
4	eggs (beaten)	4
1 c.	whole wheat bread crumbs	250 mL
1 c.	white Cheddar cheese (grated)	250 mL
2½ c.	carrots (grated)	625 mL
2 T.	pure vegetable oil	30 mL
1 T.	onion (grated)	15 mL
1 T.	parsley (chopped)	15 mL
2 t.	salt	10 mL
½ t.	pepper	2 mL

Combine milk and flour in screwtop jar; blend well. Combine remaining ingredients; mix well. Add milk mixture and stir to blend. Pour into well-greased baking dish. Bake at 350° F (175° C) for 30 to 40 minutes or until set.

Microwave: Cook on High for 15 to 20 minutes. Turn dish a quarter turn every 5 minutes.

Yield: 6 to 8 servings

Asparagus au Gratin

2 lb.	asparagus (cooked)	1 kg
2 T.	sweet butter	30 mL
1 T.	all-purpose flour	15 mL
½ t.	salt	2 mL
1 c.	light cream or milk	250 mL
½ c.	Swiss cheese (grated)	125 mL
½ c.	bread crumbs (toasted)	125 mL

Prepare asparagus. Melt butter over medium heat in saucepan. Stir in flour. Cook over low heat until golden brown. Remove from heat. Stir in salt and light cream or milk. Return to heat. Cook and stir until mixture bubbles. Add cheese. Cook until cheese melts. Place asparagus in single layer in baking dish. Pour sauce evenly over asparagus. Sprinkle with bread crumbs. Bake at 350° F (175° C) for 15 minutes or until lightly browned.

Microwave: Combine as above. Cook on Medium for 4 to 5 minutes.

Yield: 6 to 8 servings

Green Beans with Cream Cheese Sauce

2 c.	green beans (cooked and hot)	500 mL
1 T.	sweet butter	15 mL
1 c.	mushrooms (sliced)	250 mL
3-oz. pkg.	cream cheese (softened)	90-g pkg.
2 T.	milk	30 mL
1 T.	celery (chopped fine)	15 mL
½ t.	salt	2 mL

Prepare green beans. Heat butter in saucepan. Add mushrooms and sauté. Beat cream cheese until fluffy. Beat in milk, celery, and salt. Spoon mixture over hot mushrooms. Cook and stir over low heat until warm. Pour over hot, cooked green beans. Toss to coat.

Yield: 4 to 5 servings

Iowa Fries
(Homemade Potato Chips)

Potatoes (peeled and thinly sliced)

Place potato slices in large glass bowl. Cover completely with ice. Fill bowl with enough cold water to cover potato slices. Allow to chill at least 1 hour. Remove 2 c. (500 mL) potato slices. Drain and pat dry. Fry in very hot pure vegetable oil, (375° F; 190° C), until golden brown and crisp. Drain. Salt to taste. Repeat with remaining potato slices.

Potatoes of Paris

3 large	potatoes (peeled)	3 large
2 T.	sweet butter	30 mL
2 T.	parsley (chopped)	30 mL
	salt and pepper to taste	

Shape potatoes into small balls with melon baller or scoop. Parboil in salted water 3 to 4 minutes. Drain. Melt butter in skillet; add potatoes. Cook and roll until golden brown. Pour into heated serving dish. Sprinkle with parsley and salt and pepper to taste.

Yield: 4 to 5 servings

Harvard Beets

2 c.	beets (cooked and diced)	500 mL
½ c.	sugar	125 mL
½ c.	distilled white vinegar	125 mL
1 T.	cornstarch	15 mL
1 t.	salt	5 mL
2 T.	sweet butter	30 mL

Prepare beets. Combine sugar, vinegar, cornstarch, and salt in saucepan. Bring to boil. Boil and stir for 5 minutes. Add butter. Pour over beets. Cover; allow to marinate 10 minutes or refrigerate. Serve hot or cold.

Yield: 6 to 8 servings

SALADS

The Salad Bowl

4 heads	Bibb lettuce	4 heads
½ head	iceberg lettuce	½ head
2	avocados (peeled and sliced)	2
2	eggs (hard-cooked and sliced)	2
6-oz. can	artichoke hearts (chilled)	170-g can

Clean and crisp greens. Break into large pieces and place in serving bowl. Top with remaining ingredients. Cover and refrigerate. Just before serving, sprinkle with favorite dressing.

Yield: 8 to 10 servings

Shredded Carrot Salad

2 c.	carrots (shredded)	500 mL
1 small	onion (chopped)	1 small
⅓ c.	pure vegetable oil	90 mL
1 T.	lemon juice	15 mL
	lettuce leaves	

Combine all ingredients. Marinate 2 hours or overnight. Drain. Arrange on lettuce leaves.

Yield: 4 to 5 servings

Mixed Fruit Platter

1	Watermelon Jell (p. 86)	1
½	cantaloupe (peeled and sliced)	½
¼	honeydew (peeled and sliced)	¼
3	kiwis (peeled and sliced)	3
2	mangoes (peeled and sliced)	2
4	bananas (peeled and sliced in quarters)	4
10 to 12	dates	10 to 12
2 c.	whipped heavy cream	500 mL
	lemon juice	

Make Watermelon Jell in ring mold. Unmold gelatin onto center of large platter. Arrange cantaloupe slices around half of gelatin mold. Arrange honeydew slices around the other half of gelatin mold. Arrange kiwi slices on each cantaloupe slice. Arrange mango slices on edge of honeydew slices. Place banana quarters around edge of platter. Toss dates on top of fruit. Spoon whipped cream into wide-mouth glass; place in center of ring mold. Sprinkle all fresh fruit with small amount of lemon juice.

Yield: 15 to 20 servings

Cream Cheese Salad

1 env.	unflavored gelatin	1 env.
1 c.	pineapple juice	250 mL
3-oz. pkg.	cream cheese	90-g pkg.
1 c.	pineapple (crushed)	250 mL
¾ c.	whipped heavy cream	190 mL
1 c.	walnuts (pieces)	250 mL

Combine gelatin and pineapple juice in saucepan. Cook over low heat until gelatin is completely dissolved. Remove from heat. Add cream cheese and stir until melted. Refrigerate until syrupy. Stir in crushed pineapple, whipped cream, and walnuts. Pour into serving bowl or mold. Refrigerate until firm.

Yield: 6 to 8 servings

Colorful Salad Bowl

1 small head	iceberg lettuce	1 small head
1/4 bunch	curly endive	1/4 bunch
1	grapefruit (peeled and sectioned)	1
7	radishes (sliced)	7
24	carrot curls	24
12	ripe olives (pitted and halved)	12
3	eggs (hard-cooked and sliced)	3
2 slices	onion (broken up into rings)	2 slices

Tear greens into bite-size pieces. Arrange grapefruit, vegetables, and eggs on top of greens. Toss at table with favorite dressing.

Yield: 8 to 10 servings

Autumn Salad

2 c.	Grapefruit Gelatin (p. 87)	500 mL
2 c.	carrots (grated)	500 mL
1 c.	cranberries (chopped)	250 mL

Prepare Grapefruit Gelatin, but chill only until slightly thickened. Add carrots and cranberries. Stir to blend. Chill until firm.

Yield: 4 c. (1000 mL)

Sweet Sauerkraut Salad

2 c.	sauerkraut	500 mL
1/2 c.	sugar	125 mL
1/2 c.	celery (sliced)	125 mL
1/2 c.	carrots (shredded)	125 mL
1/4 c.	onion (diced)	60 mL

Combine sauerkraut and sugar. Allow to rest 30 minutes. Add remaining ingredients. Cover. Refrigerate overnight.

Yield: 3 c. (750 mL)

Pineapple Supreme

1 c.	pineapple juice	250 mL
½ c.	sugar	125 mL
2 T.	cornstarch	30 mL
1 T.	sweet butter	15 mL
½ c.	Marshmallow Creme (p. 158)	125 mL
2 c.	pineapple (chunks)	500 mL
½ c.	celery (chunks)	125 mL
3	pears (peeled and cut into chunks)	3
½ c.	nutmeats (not almonds)	125 mL
2 c.	whipped heavy cream	500 mL

Combine pineapple juice, sugar, and cornstarch in saucepan. Cook and stir over medium heat until clear. Remove from heat. Add butter and Marshmallow Creme. Stir to completely dissolve. Pour over pineapple chunks. Allow to cool. Stir in chunks of celery and pears. Fold in nutmeats and whipped cream.

Yield: 8 to 10 servings

Confetti Cabbage Slaw

3 c.	cabbage (finely shredded)	750 mL
1 c.	carrots (shredded)	250 mL
½	onion (thinly sliced)	½
10	radishes (chopped)	10
½ c.	celery (sliced)	125 mL
2 T.	sugar	15 mL
1 t.	salt	5 mL
dash	pepper	dash
1 c.	Slaw Dressing (p. 98)	250 mL

Place vegetables in serving bowl. Sprinkle with sugar, salt and pepper. Mix lightly. Pour Slaw Dressing over salad and toss with fork.

Yield: 5 to 6 servings

Tuna Potato Salad

⅓ c.	pure vegetable oil	90 mL
2 T.	lemon juice	30 mL
1 T.	distilled white vinegar	15 mL
1 T.	sugar	15 mL
½ t.	garlic powder	2 mL
¼ t.	salt	1 mL
½ t.	pepper	2 mL
16-oz. can	whole green beans (drained)	500-g can
3 c.	potatoes (cooked and diced)	750 mL
7-oz. can	tuna chunks (drained)	210-g can
1	onion (sliced thin)	1
½ c.	ripe olives (sliced)	125 mL
½ c.	black olives (sliced)	125 mL

Combine oil, lemon juice, vinegar, sugar, garlic powder, salt, and pepper in salad bowl; stir to blend. Add remaining ingredients. Toss lightly; cover and chill thoroughly.

Yield: 4 to 5 servings

Vegetable Salad Mold

2 c.	Grapefruit Gelatin (p. 87)	500 mL
1 c.	carrots (shredded)	250 mL
1 c.	celery (chopped fine)	250 mL
¼ c.	onion (chopped fine)	60 mL
½ c.	radishes (sliced)	125 mL
1½ c.	spinach (rinsed and torn)	375 mL
	Cream Mayonnaise (p. 94)	

Prepare Grapefruit Gelatin, but chill only until slightly thickened. Arrange carrots in bottom of well-greased 2-qt. (2-L) gelatin mold. Carefully pour ½ c. (125 mL) of the slightly thickened gelatin over carrots. Layer celery, onion, radishes, and then spinach over gelatin. Carefully pour over remaining gelatin. Chill until firm (at least 5 hours). Unmold on chilled serving plate. Serve with Cream Mayonnaise.

Yield: 10 to 12 servings

Banana Grapefruit Nut Salad

⅓ c.	pure vegetable oil	90 mL
2 T.	lemon juice	30 mL
1 T.	sugar	15 mL
½ t.	dry mustard	2 mL
½ t.	salt	2 mL
¼ t.	pepper	1 mL
2	grapefruit	2
4	bananas (sliced)	4
3 c.	Bibb lettuce (rinsed and torn)	750 mL
⅓ c.	pecans (halved)	90 mL

Combine oil, lemon juice, sugar, dry mustard, salt, and pepper in salad bowl. Stir to blend. Peel and remove membrane from grapefruit sections. Fold grapefruit sections and bananas into dressing in salad bowl; toss lightly. Chill. Just before serving, add Bibb lettuce and toss. Top with pecan halves.

Yield: 4 to 5 servings

Spinach-Egg Salad

1 qt.	spinach (rinsed and torn)	1 L
4	eggs (hard-cooked and sliced)	4
½ c.	pure or homemade Mayonnaise (p. 95)	125 mL
¼ c.	Chili Sauce (p. 91)	60 mL
1 T.	onion (grated)	15 mL
5 slices	bacon (fried and crumbled)	5 slices

Prepare spinach and eggs. Combine Mayonnaise, Chili Sauce, and onion in small bowl; stir to blend. Chill. Place torn spinach in salad bowl. Top with egg slices. At serving time, pour chilled dressing over spinach-egg mixture. Sprinkle with crumbled bacon.

Yield: 4 to 5 servings

Grapefruit-Chicken Salad

2 c.	Grapefruit Gelatin (p. 87)	500 mL
1 c.	grapefruit sections (drained)	250 mL
2 c.	chicken (cooked and cooled)	500 mL
½ c.	walnuts (chopped)	125 mL
½ c.	celery (chopped)	125 mL

Prepare Grapefruit Gelatin, but chill only until slightly thickened. Add remaining ingredients. Chill until firm.

Yield: 4 c. (1000 mL)

Three-Bean Salad

2 c.	green beans (cooked)	500 mL
2 c.	yellow beans (cooked)	500 mL
2 c.	kidney beans (cooked)	500 mL
1 c.	distilled white vinegar	250 mL
1 c.	sugar	250 mL
½ c.	pure vegetable oil	125 mL
1	onion (chopped)	1

Drain beans; set aside. Combine vinegar, sugar, and oil in saucepan. Cook until sugar is dissolved. Pour over beans. Stir in chopped onion; cover. Refrigerate until completely chilled.

Yield: 6 c. (1500 mL)

Watermelon Jell

1 env.	unflavored gelatin	1 env.
1 T.	sugar	15 mL
¼ c.	water (boiling)	60 mL
1½ c.	watermelon juice	375 mL

Combine gelatin and sugar in mixing bowl. Add boiling water; stir to completely dissolve. Cool slightly; add watermelon juice. Refrigerate until firm.

Yield: 4 to 5 servings

Lime Sherbet Jell

2 env.	unflavored gelatin	2 env.
⅓ c.	sugar	90 mL
1 c.	water (boiling)	250 mL
½ c.	lime juice	125 mL
2 c.	lime sherbet	500 mL
1 c.	whipped heavy cream	250 mL

Combine gelatin and sugar in mixing bowl. Add boiling water; stir to completely dissolve. Add lime juice. Refrigerate until syrupy. Whip until fluffy; beat in sherbet. Fold in whipped cream. Pour into serving bowl or mold. Refrigerate until set.

Yield: 8 to 10 servings

Grapefruit Gelatin

1	grapefruit	1
1 env.	unflavored gelatin	1 env.
2 T.	sugar	30 mL
2 T.	honey	30 mL

Squeeze juice and pulp from grapefruit; strain, if desired, and reserve the juice. Peel rind from grapefruit. Combine 1 c. (250 mL) water with grapefruit rind in saucepan. Boil 5 minutes. Strain; throw away rind. Add this liquid to reserved grapefruit juice and add enough water to make 2 c. (500 mL). Pour back into saucepan. Bring to boil. Combine gelatin, sugar, and honey in mixing bowl; add boiling grapefruit juice. Stir to completely dissolve. Chill until firm.

Yield: 2 c. (500 mL)

Lime Gelatin

1 env.	unflavored gelatin	1 env.
1 c.	water	250 mL
½ c.	sugar	125 mL
¼ c.	lime juice	60 mL
	peel of 1 lime, cut up (optional)	
	pure or homemade food coloring (p. 20)	

Combine all ingredients in saucepan. Cook over low heat (DO NOT BOIL) until gelatin and sugar are dissolved. Remove from heat. (Strain if peel is used.) Pour into serving bowl. Refrigerate until firm.

Yield: 4 to 5 servings

Lemon Gelatin

1 env.	unflavored gelatin	1 env.
1 c.	water	250 mL
⅓ c.	sugar	90 mL
½ c.	lemon juice	125 mL
	peel of 1 lemon, cut up (optional)	
	pure or homemade food coloring (p. 20)	

Combine all ingredients in saucepan. Cook over low heat (DO NOT BOIL) until gelatin and sugar are dissolved. Remove from heat. (Strain if peel is used.) Pour into serving bowl. Refrigerate until firm.

Yield: 4 to 5 servings

SAUCES AND SALAD DRESSINGS

Tartar Sauce

1 c.	pure or homemade Mayonnaise (p. 95)	250 mL
2 T.	lemon juice	30 mL
1	egg (finely chopped)	1
1 T.	green olives (finely chopped)	15 mL
1 t.	onion (finely chopped)	5 mL
1 t.	parsley (finely chopped)	5 mL

Combine all ingredients; stir to blend. Refrigerate and allow to rest 1 hour before serving.

Yield: 1 c. (250 mL)

English Hard Sauce

½ c.	sweet butter	125 mL
1 c.	confectioners' sugar (sifted)	250 mL
1 t.	pure vanilla extract	5 mL
¼ c.	heavy cream	60 mL

Cream the butter until soft; gradually add sugar. Beat until well blended. Beat in vanilla extract and heavy cream. Chill thoroughly.

Yield: 1½ c. (375 mL)

White Sauce

3 T.	sweet butter	45 mL
3 T.	all-purpose flour	45 mL
1½ c.	milk	325 mL
1 t.	onion salt	5 mL
½ t.	thyme	2 mL
¼ t.	pepper	1 mL

Melt butter in skillet over low heat. Add flour. Cook to make a paste. Gradually add milk, stirring continuously. Cook until desired thickness. Remove from heat; add seasonings. Stir to blend.

Yield: 1½ c. (325 mL)

Italian Sauce

2 to 2½ c.	water	500 to 625 mL
½ c.	red beans	125 mL
1	bay leaf	1
¼ c.	distilled white vinegar	60 mL
1 T.	lemon juice	15 mL
¼ c.	onion (chopped)	60 mL
2 T.	parsley (chopped)	30 mL
2 t.	oregano	10 mL
1 t.	garlic powder	5 mL

Combine water, red beans, and bay leaf in saucepan. Bring to boil. Simmer for 1½ to 2 hours or until beans are tender. (Add extra water if needed.) Remove bay leaf and drain. Cool slightly. Pour beans into blender; add vinegar and lemon juice. Blend to puree. Return puree to saucepan. Add remaining ingredients and enough water to achieve desired thickness. Cook over low heat.

Yield: 1½ c. (375 mL)

Chili Sauce

1	yellow squash (pulp)	1
1	pear (peeled and cubed)	1
1	onion (cubed)	1
½ c.	water	125 mL
1 c.	distilled white vinegar	250 mL
1 c.	sugar	250 mL
2 t.	salt	10 mL
¼ t. each	paprika, cinnamon, allspice	1 mL each
	optional: pure or homemade food coloring (p. 20)	

Combine squash, pear, onion, and water in blender or food processor. Whip until smooth. (Add extra water if needed.) Pour into saucepan; add vinegar and sugar. Stir and cook over medium heat until thick. Stir in seasonings. Cook 2 minutes. Add food coloring, if desired.

Yield: 2½ to 3 c. (650 to 750 mL)

Mock Applesauce

24	pure or homemade Saltine Crackers (p. 102)	24
1½ c.	sugar	375 mL
1½ c.	water	375 mL
½ c.	dates (cut into small pieces)	125 mL
2 t.	cream of tartar	10 mL
1 T.	sweet butter	15 mL
1 t.	cinnamon	5 mL
½ t.	nutmeg	2 mL

Crumble Saltine Crackers in bowl. Combine sugar, water, and dates in saucepan. Bring to boil. Remove from heat; allow to rest 5 minutes. Add remaining ingredients. Return to heat. Simmer 2 minutes or until well blended. Pour over crumbled crackers. Stir to blend; add extra water if needed. Chill.

Yield: 1½ c. (375 mL)

Hollandaise Sauce

1 T.	all-purpose flour	15 mL
½ t.	salt	2 mL
1 c.	water	250 mL
½ c.	sweet butter	125 mL
4	egg yolks	4
½ c.	fish stock	125 mL
2 T.	lemon juice	30 mL

Combine flour, salt, and water in screwtop jar; shake to blend. Pour into saucepan and bring to a boil. Remove from heat. Stir in butter and allow to melt. Beat egg yolks, one at a time, into flour mixture. Stir in fish stock. Return to heat. Beat until desired thickness. Remove from heat. Stir in lemon juice.

Yield: 1 c. (250 mL)

Milk Chocolate Sauce

¾ c.	sugar	190 mL
⅓ c.	pure cocoa	90 mL
1 t.	salt	5 mL
¼ c.	water	60 mL
½ c.	light cream	125 mL
1 t.	pure vanilla extract	5 mL

Combine sugar, cocoa, salt, and water in saucepan. Stir and cook over medium heat until mixture comes to full boil; reduce heat. Stir and cook to soft ball stage (234° F; 112° C)—about 8 minutes. Remove from heat. Beat in cream and vanilla extract.

Microwave: Combine as above in large glass bowl. Cook on Medium for 5 minutes; stir; cook 5 to 6 minutes to soft ball stage. Continue with remaining instructions.

Yield: 1 c. (250 mL)

Date Nut Sauce

½ c.	dates (chopped fine)	125 mL
½ c.	honey	125 mL
½ c.	water	125 mL
¼ c.	brown sugar	60 mL
½ t.	pure vanilla extract	2 mL
¼ c.	pecans (chopped)	60 mL

Combine dates, honey, water, and brown sugar in saucepan. Stir and cook over medium heat until mixture comes to full boil. Reduce heat; stir and cook 2 minutes. Remove from heat. Add vanilla extract and pecans.

Microwave: Combine as above in large glass bowl. Cook on High for 5 minutes; stir every 2 minutes. Add vanilla extract and pecans.

Yield: 1½ c. (325 mL)

Butterscotch Syrup

1 c.	brown sugar (packed)	250 mL
1 c.	corn syrup	250 mL
½ c.	milk	125 mL
2 T.	sweet butter	30 mL
½ t.	salt	2 mL
1 t.	pure vanilla extract	5 mL

Combine brown sugar, corn syrup, milk, butter, and salt in saucepan. Stir and cook over medium heat until mixture comes to full boil. Reduce heat. Stir and simmer 5 minutes. Remove from heat. Stir in vanilla extract.

Microwave: Combine as above in large glass bowl. Cook on Medium for 8 minutes; stir every 2 minutes. Stir in vanilla extract.

Yield: 1½ c. (325 mL)

Banana Syrup

1 qt.	sugar	1 L
2 c.	water	500 mL
2 lb.	bananas (peeled and sliced)	1 kg
¼ c.	lemon juice	60 mL
1 t.	pure vanilla extract	5 mL

Boil sugar and water together for 4 to 5 minutes. Combine bananas and lemon juice in food processor or blender. Blend until smooth. Add to sugar mixture. Boil over low heat, stirring constantly, until desired thickness. Remove from heat; stir in vanilla extract. Pour into sterilized jars. Seal.

Yield: 3 c. (750 mL)

Chocolate Syrup

½ c.	sugar	125 mL
½ c.	water	125 mL
¼ c.	corn syrup	60 mL
2 T.	pure cocoa	30 mL
¼ t.	salt	1 mL
½ t.	pure vanilla extract	2 mL

Combine sugar, water, and corn syrup in a saucepan. Cook and stir to thread stage (230° F; 100° C). Remove from heat. Add cocoa and salt; stir to dissolve. Add vanilla extract. Cool.

Microwave: Combine as above in large glass bowl. Cook on High 3 to 4 minutes or to thread stage. Continue with remaining instructions.

Yield: ½ c. (125 mL)

Cream Mayonnaise

1 c.	whipped heavy cream	250 mL
1 c.	Mayonnaise (p. 95)	250 mL

Fold whipped cream into Mayonnaise thoroughly. Chill.

Yield: 2 c. (500 mL)

Mayonnaise

2	eggs	2
2 T.	flour	30 mL
1 t.	salt	5 mL
1 t.	dry mustard	5 mL
¼ c.	distilled white vinegar	60 mL
2 T.	lemon juice	30 mL
½ c.	sugar	125 mL
½ c.	water	125 mL
1 c.	pure vegetable oil	250 mL

Combine eggs, flour, salt, dry mustard, vinegar, lemon juice, sugar, and water in saucepan. Cook over low heat until thickened. Remove from heat. Gradually add oil, beating until smooth. Store in covered container in refrigerator.

Yield: 2 c. (500 mL)

Creamy French Dressing

½ c.	French Dressing (p. 99)	125 mL
3-oz. pkg.	cream cheese (softened)	90-g pkg.
2 T.	parsley (chopped)	30 mL
1 t.	salt	5 mL
¼ c.	pure vegetable oil	60 mL
2 T.	lemon juice	30 mL
1 t.	paprika	5 mL

Combine all ingredients in blender or food processor. Blend thoroughly. Store in tightly covered jar in refrigerator. Shake well before using.

Yield: 1 c. (250 mL)

Italian Dressing

1 c.	pure vegetable oil	250 mL
⅓ c.	distilled white vinegar	90 mL
½ c.	onion (finely chopped)	125 mL
¼ c.	parsley (finely chopped)	60 mL
2 t.	salt	10 mL
1 t.	garlic powder	5 mL
1 t.	oregano	5 mL
½ t.	pepper	2 mL
¼ t.	thyme	1 mL
¼ t.	rosemary	1 mL

Combine all ingredients in tightly covered jar or bottle. Allow to rest 24 hours. Shake well before using.

Yield: 1½ c. (375 mL)

Honey Fruit Dressing

⅔ c.	sugar	160 mL
1 t.	dry mustard	5 mL
1 t.	paprika	5 mL
1 t.	celery seeds	5 mL
¼ t.	salt	1 mL
⅓ c.	honey	90 mL
5 T.	distilled white vinegar	75 mL
1 T.	lemon juice	15 mL
1 t.	onion (grated)	5 mL
1 c.	pure vegetable oil	250 mL

Combine sugar, dry mustard, paprika, celery seeds, salt, honey, vinegar, lemon juice, and grated onion. Beat to blend. Gradually add oil, beating constantly. Chill.

Yield: 1½ c. (375 mL)

Garlic Dressing

1 c.	pure vegetable oil	250 mL
1 clove	garlic (minced)	1 clove
¼ c.	distilled white vinegar	60 mL
1 t.	salt	5 mL
½ t.	white pepper	2 mL
½ t.	celery salt	2 mL
¼ t.	cayenne pepper	1 mL
¼ t.	dry mustard	1 mL

Combine ingredients in screwtop jar. Cover. Refrigerate 2 to 3 hours. Shake vigorously before using.

Yield: 1¼ c. (310 mL)

Fruit Salad Mayonnaise

1 c.	Mayonnaise (p. 95)	250 mL
⅓ c.	pineapple juice	90 mL
½ t.	lemon rind (grated)	2 mL

Stir ingredients together thoroughly. Store in tightly covered jar in refrigerator.

Yield: 1⅓ c. (340 mL)

Thousand Island Dressing

1 c.	Tomatoless Ketchup (p. 98)	250 mL
½ c.	Mayonnaise (p. 95)	125 mL
2 T.	parsley (chopped)	30 mL
2 T.	celery (chopped)	30 mL
2 T.	lemon juice	30 mL
1 t.	paprika	5 mL

Beat or blend ingredients together thoroughly. Store in tightly covered jar in refrigerator.

Yield: 2 c. (500 mL)

Tomatoless Ketchup

2 c.	yellow squash (peeled and cubed)	500 mL
⅓ c.	distilled white vinegar	90 mL
1 small	onion (cubed)	1 small
½ c.	white corn syrup	125 mL
¼ t.	garlic powder	1 mL
¼ t.	mustard seeds	1 mL
¼ t.	cinnamon	1 mL
¼ c.	beet juice food coloring (p. 20)	60 mL
2 t.	optional: spinach food coloring (p. 20)	10 mL

Put all ingredients in blender or food processor. Blend until smooth. Pour into saucepan; cook over medium heat to desired consistency.

To Can or Preserve: Pack in clean, hot jars. Leave ½ in. (1.25 cm) of headspace. Close the jars and process in boiling-water bath 30 minutes for 2-c. (500-mL) jars.

To Freeze: Allow to cool. Pack in clean freezer containers. Leave 1 in. (2.5 cm) of headspace. Cover.

Yield: 2 c. (500 mL)

Slaw Dressing

⅓ c.	all-purpose flour	90 mL
1 t.	sugar	5 mL
1 t.	salt	5 mL
½ t.	dry mustard	2 mL
1 c.	water (cold)	250 mL
¼ c.	distilled white vinegar	60 mL
1 T.	sweet butter	15 mL
1	egg (slightly beaten)	1
1 c.	pure vegetable oil	250 mL

Combine flour, sugar, salt, and dry mustard in saucepan. Gradually blend in cold water and vinegar. Cook and stir over medium heat until mixture is smooth and slightly thickened. Remove from heat; stir in butter. Slowly beat hot mixture into egg; beat in vegetable oil.

Yield: 2 c. (500 mL)

Creamy Bleu Cheese Dressing

1 c.	pure vegetable oil	250 mL
⅓ c.	distilled white vinegar	90 mL
⅓ c.	bleu cheese	90 mL
1 t.	bay leaf (ground)	5 mL
1 T.	onion (chopped)	15 mL
½ t.	salt	2 mL
¼ t.	pepper	1 mL

Combine all ingredients in blender or food processor. Blend thoroughly. Store in tightly covered jar in refrigerator. Shake well before using.

Yield: 1½ c. (375 mL)

French Dressing

1 c.	pure vegetable oil	250 mL
½ c.	Tomatoless Ketchup (p. 98)	125 mL
⅓ c.	distilled white vinegar	90 mL
2 t.	onion salt	10 mL
1 t.	mustard seeds	5 mL
1 t.	bay leaf (ground)	5 mL
1 t.	garlic powder	5 mL
¼ t.	pepper	1 mL

Combine all ingredients in blender or food processor. Blend thoroughly. Store in tightly covered jar in refrigerator. Shake well before using.

Yield: 2 c. (500 mL)

BREADS, PANCAKES, AND PASTAS

Cinnamon Rolls

1 pkg.	yeast	1 pkg.
½ c.	water (lukewarm)	125 mL
1 c.	milk (scalded)	250 mL
¼ c.	shortening	60 mL
¼ c.	sugar	60 mL
1 t.	salt	5 mL
1	egg	1
3 to 4 c.	all-purpose flour	750 to 1000 mL
¼ c.	sweet butter (melted)	60 mL
½ c.	sugar	125 mL
2 t.	cinnamon	10 mL

Soften yeast in lukewarm water; set aside. Whip milk, shortening, ¼ c. (60 mL) sugar, the salt, and egg. Cool to lukewarm. Add 1 c. (250 mL) of the flour; beat well. Beat in yeast mixture. Gradually add remaining flour to make a soft dough. Cover. Allow to rise in warm place until double in size. Turn dough out on floured surface. Roll to 18 × 10-in. (46 × 25-cm) rectangle. Spread melted butter over entire surface. Sprinkle with ½ c. (125 mL) sugar and the cinnamon. Roll the dough up from the 18-in. (46-cm) side; seal ends. Cut into 18 pieces. Place in two well-greased 9-in. (23-cm) round pans. Cover. Allow to rise until double in size. Bake at 375° F (190° C) for 20 to 25 minutes. Remove from pans. Frost if desired.

Yield: 18 rolls

Convenience Mix

10 c.	all-purpose flour	2500 mL
1 c.	pure dry milk	250 mL
½ c.	baking powder	125 mL
1 T.	salt	15 mL
2½ t.	cream of tartar	12 mL
2 c.	pure solid shortening	500 mL

Place all ingredients in large bowl. Cut shortening into dry mixture until mix is consistency of cornmeal. Store in covered container. Mix will last indefinitely in refrigerator; 1 to 2 months at room temperature.

Yield: 3 qt. (3 L)

Convenience Muffins

2 c.	Convenience Mix (p. 101)	500 mL
2 T.	sugar	30 mL
¾ c.	milk or water	190 mL
1	egg	1

Combine ingredients; stir to blend. Fill well-greased muffin tins ⅔ full. Bake at 350° F (175° C) for 20 minutes.

Yield: 1 dozen muffins

Convenience Waffles

2 c.	Convenience Mix (p. 101)	500 mL
1¼ c.	milk	310 mL
2	eggs	2
2 T.	pure vegetable oil	30 mL

Mix ingredients thoroughly. Bake on hot waffle iron until golden brown.

Yield: 4–5 waffles

Convenience Pancakes

2 c.	Convenience Mix (p. 101)	500 mL
1½ c.	milk	325 mL
1	egg	1

Mix ingredients thoroughly. Fry on hot griddle.

Yield: 10–12 pancakes

Convenience Biscuits or Dumplings

| 2 c. | Convenience Mix (p. 101) | 500 mL |
| ⅔ c. | milk or water | 160 mL |

Biscuits: Combine ingredients; stir to blend. Drop by spoonfuls onto greased cookie sheet, or knead and roll out ½ in. (1 cm) thick; cut with biscuit cutter. Bake at 350° F (175° C) for 10 to 12 minutes.

Dumplings: Prepare as above. Drop dough by spoonfuls into boiling stew, soup, or water. Cover. Reduce heat and simmer 10 to 15 minutes.

Yield: 1 dozen biscuits or dumplings

Saltine Crackers

1 qt.	all-purpose flour	1 L
1 t.	baking powder	5 mL
¾ c.	shortening	190 mL
1	egg (slightly beaten)	1
1 c.	water	250 mL
	salt to taste	

Combine flour, baking powder, and shortening. Mix to crumb consistency. Add egg and water. Stir to thoroughly mix. Turn out onto floured surface. Roll very thin. Cut into squares of desired size. Prick with fork. Salt to taste. Place on ungreased cookie tins. Bake at 375° F (190° C) for 10 to 12 minutes or until crisp.

Yield: 100–125 crackers

Refrigerator Sweet Dough

2 pkg.	yeast	2 pkg.
1 c.	water (warm)	250 mL
¼ c.	pure solid shortening	60 mL
1 c.	pure evaporated milk	250 mL
½ c.	sugar	125 mL
1½ t.	salt	7 mL
2	eggs	2
6 c.	all-purpose flour	1500 mL

Sprinkle yeast on warm water in large bread bowl. Stir to dissolve. Add shortening; stir until melted. Add evaporated milk, sugar, salt, and eggs. Beat until well blended. Beat in 3 c. (750 mL) of the flour until smooth. Stir in remaining flour. Turn out onto lightly floured board. Knead 8 to 10 minutes or until flour is worked in and dough is smooth. Store in large covered container in refrigerator. When ready to use, pinch off enough dough for recipe. Allow to rest 10 minutes before using in recipe.

Yield: Dough for 2 to 3 coffeecakes or 3 dozen rolls

Peanut Butter Surprises

¼ recipe	Refrigerator Sweet Dough (p. 103)	¼ recipe
½ c.	pure peanut butter	125 mL
	pure vegetable oil	
¼ c.	confectioners' sugar (sifted)	60 mL
¼ c.	peanuts (powdered)	60 mL

Roll out dough ¼ in. (.62 cm) thick. Cut with 2-in. (5-cm) biscuit cutter. Place 1 T. (15 mL) peanut butter in center of each circle. Fold in half; seal edge well. Place on well-greased cookie sheet. Allow to double in size. Heat pure vegetable oil to 375° F (190° C). Dip slotted turner in hot oil, then carefully remove dough from cookie sheet. Fry until golden brown. Turn frequently. Drain. Mix sugar and peanut powder in bowl. Roll hot Surprises in sugar-peanut mixture.

Yield: 10 to 12 Surprises

Doughnuts

1 c.	milk	250 mL
1 c.	sugar	250 mL
1	egg	1
¼ c.	shortening (melted)	60 mL
½ t.	salt	2 mL
1 t.	nutmeg	5 mL
4 t.	baking powder	20 mL
3 to 4 c.	all-purpose flour	750 to 1000 mL
	oil for deep-fat frying	

Beat milk, sugar, egg, shortening, salt, and nutmeg until well blended. Stir in baking powder and enough flour to roll—3½ c. (875 mL). Turn out on lightly floured surface. Roll out ½ in. (1.3 cm) thick. Cut with doughnut cutter. Fry in hot oil, 350° F (175° C), until golden brown. Turn often.

Yield: 2 to 2½ dozen doughnuts

Filled Long Johns or Doughnuts

¼ recipe	Refrigerator Sweet Dough (p. 103)	¼ recipe
	pure vegetable oil	
½ c.	pure favorite jelly	125 mL
½ c.	Quick White or Chocolate Frosting (p. 122)	125 mL

Roll out dough ½ in. (1.25 cm) thick. Cut into rectangles or circles. Place on well-greased cookie sheet; cover. Allow to double in size. Heat pure vegetable oil to 375° F (190° C). Dip slotted turner into hot oil, then carefully remove doughnuts from cookie sheet. Fry until golden brown. Turn frequently. Drain and cool completely. Slit side of doughnut with sharp knife. Turn knife to open a space in the center. Using a spoon or pastry tube, fill center with jelly. Frost with Quick White or Chocolate Frosting.

Yield: 8 to 10 Long Johns or doughnuts

Corn Bread or Pancakes

1 c.	cornmeal	250 mL
1 c.	all-purpose flour	250 mL
1 c.	milk	250 mL
¼ c.	sugar	60 mL
¼ c.	pure vegetable oil	60 mL
1½ T.	baking powder	25 mL
1	egg	1

Combine all ingredients. Beat just until smooth. Pour into well-greased 8-in. (20-cm) square pan. Bake at 425° F (220° C) for 20 to 25 minutes or fry on hot griddle.

Yield: 1 cake or 24 pancakes

Crumb Topping

1 c.	flour	250 mL
½ c.	brown sugar	125 mL
¼ c.	pure solid shortening	60 mL
½ t.	baking soda	2 mL

Combine all ingredients in bowl. Work with fork and knife or pastry blender into crumbs the size of peas. Sprinkle over desired pastry.

Yield: 1½ c. (375 mL)

Crisp Topping or Crust

6 c.	bread crumbs (fine)	1500 mL
3 c.	brown sugar (packed)	750 mL
3 c.	all-purpose flour	750 mL
2 c.	pure dry milk	500 mL
1 lb.	sweet butter	500 g
1 t.	cinnamon	5 mL
1 t.	salt	5 mL

Combine all ingredients in large bowl or pan. Work in butter until mixture is fine crumbs. Store in large covered container; freeze.

Yield: 4 qt. (4 L)

Pear Pancakes

2 c.	all-purpose flour	500 mL
2 c.	milk	500 mL
2	eggs	2
2 T.	sweet butter (melted)	30 mL
3	pears	3
¾ to 1 c.	sugar	190 to 250 mL

Combine flour, milk, eggs, and butter; beat only until smooth. Allow to rest 5 to 10 minutes or until slightly thickened. Peel, core, and slice pears. Heat lightly greased skillet or griddle. For each pancake, spoon 2 to 3 T. (30 to 45 mL) batter onto skillet or griddle. Fry until partially set. Top with sliced pears. When bottom of pancake is browned, flip; sprinkle with sugar. When thoroughly cooked, flip pancake onto hot serving plate; sprinkle with more sugar.

Yield: 10 to 12 pancakes

Rye Bread

1 pkg.	yeast	1 pkg.
½ c.	water (lukewarm)	125 mL
4 t.	salt	20 mL
4 t.	shortening	20 mL
1 t.	sugar	5 mL
1 T.	caraway seeds	15 mL
2 T.	unsulphured molasses	30 mL
2 c.	potato water (lukewarm)	500 mL
2 c.	rye flour	500 mL
	all-purpose flour	

Dissolve yeast in lukewarm water. Combine salt, shortening, sugar, caraway seeds, molasses, and lukewarm potato water; stir in rye flour. Add yeast mixture. Stir to blend. Knead in small amount of all-purpose flour until dough is smooth. Cover. Allow to rise in warm place. Punch down; form into two round loaves. Place on greased baking sheet. Cover. Allow to rise until double in size. Bake at 350° F (175° C) for 45 to 50 minutes.

Yield: 2 loaves

Honey Graham Crackers

⅔ c.	pure solid shortening	160 mL
½ c.	pure honey	125 mL
2¼ c.	graham flour	560 mL
2 t.	baking powder	10 mL
¼ t.	salt	1 mL
½ c.	sweet light cream	125 mL

Cream shortening and honey until light and fluffy. Combine flour, baking powder, and salt in sifter. Sift flour mixture and cream alternately into honey mixture. Stir to blend well. Roll out thinly on lightly floured board. Cut into 2-in. (5-cm) squares. Prick with fork. Place on ungreased cookie sheets. Bake at 375° F (190° C) for 6 to 8 minutes or until brown. Cool on rack.

Yield: 90 to 100 crackers

Cream Waffles with Mango Topping

1½ c.	all-purpoose flour	375 mL
½ t.	salt	2 mL
1 c.	ice water	250 mL
2 c.	heavy cream	500 mL
2 T.	sweet butter (melted)	30 mL
1 lb.	mangoes (sliced)	500 g
	additional whipped cream	

Beat flour, salt, ice water, and ½ c. (125 mL) of the heavy cream until smooth. Fold melted butter into batter. Whip remaining cream until stiff or thick. Fold into batter. Bake on hot waffle iron until golden brown and crispy. Cool waffles, in single layer, on cake rack. Top with mango slices and additional whipped cream.

Yield: 6 waffles

Homemade Cereal

3 qt.	rolled oats	3 L
1½ qt.	wheat germ	1.5 L
1½ qt.	unsweetened coconut (shredded)	1.5 L
1 c.	sweet butter (melted)	250 mL
1 t.	salt	5 mL

Combine ingredients; mix together thoroughly. Place on two large cookie tins. Bake at 350° F (175° C) until lightly browned. Stir occasionally. Store in airtight container.

Yield: 6 qt. (6 L)

Cornmeal Dumplings

¼ c.	all-purpose flour	60 mL
1 t.	baking powder	5 mL
½ t.	salt	2 mL
1 c.	cornmeal	250 mL
1	egg	1
½ c.	milk	125 mL
1 T.	sweet butter (melted)	15 mL

Sift together flour, baking powder, salt, and cornmeal. Add egg, milk, and melted butter. Drop by spoonfuls onto stew. Cover. Cook 15 minutes.

Yield: 10 to 14 dumplings

Graham Cracker Pie Shell

1½ c.	Honey Graham Cracker crumbs (p. 107)	375 mL
¼ c.	sugar	60 mL
¼ c.	sweet butter (melted)	60 mL

Combine Honey Graham Cracker crumbs and sugar; blend in butter. Press evenly onto sides and bottom of well-greased 9-in. (23-cm) pie or cake pan. Chill until firm.

Yield: One 9-in. (23-cm) graham cracker pie shell

Graham-Nuts Cereal

2 c.	milk	500 mL
1 T.	lemon juice	15 mL
1 qt.	graham flour	1 L
1 c.	unsulphured molasses	250 mL
1 t.	baking soda	5 mL
1 t.	salt	5 mL

Mix milk and lemon juice. Stir and allow to sour 10 minutes. Combine remaining ingredients. Pour in milk; mix thoroughly. Pour into greased baking pan. Bake at 350° F (175° C) for 30 minutes. Break into small pieces. Return to oven until toasted, about 10 minutes. Store in airtight container.

Yield: 1 qt. (1 L)

Homemade Noodles

1	egg (slightly beaten)	1
1 T.	shortening	15 mL
2 t.	milk	10 mL
¼ t.	salt	2 mL
¼ t.	baking powder	2 mL
1¼ c.	flour	310 mL

Combine all ingredients. Stir to blend. Turn out on lightly floured board. Roll out ⅛ in. (3 mm) thick; cut to desired lengths and widths. Cook in boiling salted water, or dry and store in refrigerator.

Yield: 3 c. (750 mL)

CAKES

Banana Gingerbread

½ c.	pure solid shortening	125 mL
½ c.	sugar	125 mL
1	egg	1
½ c.	unsulphured molasses	125 mL
1½ c.	all-purpose flour	375 mL
¾ t.	salt	4 mL
1 t.	baking soda	5 mL
½ t.	ginger	2 mL
½ t.	cinnamon	2 mL
½ c.	water (boiling)	125 mL
1 recipe	Banana Spread (p. 122)	1 recipe

Beat shortening until soft. Gradually add sugar; beat until light and fluffy. Beat in egg and molasses. Sift together flour, salt, baking soda, and spices. Add to molasses mixture alternately with boiling water. Beat well after each addition. Pour into well-greased, 8-in. (20-cm) square pan. Bake at 350° F (175° C) for 40 minutes or until toothpick comes out clean. To serve, split gingerbread in half horizontally. Cover bottom half with ½ of Banana Spread. Replace top. Frost top half with remaining Banana Spread. Garnish with fresh sliced banana and walnut pieces.

Microwave: Cook on Low 7 minutes. Increase temperature to High and cook 3 to 4 minutes or until toothpick comes out clean. Fill and frost as above.

Yield: 1 cake (9 servings)

Carrot Quick Cake

1 c.	all-purpose flour	250 mL
½ c.	sugar	125 mL
½ c.	carrots (cooked and mashed)	125 mL
½ c.	milk	125 mL
¼ c.	pure vegetable oil	60 mL
1	egg	1
½ t. each	baking soda, cinnamon, salt	2 mL each

Combine all ingredients in ungreased 9 × 9-in. (23 × 23-cm) pan. Stir to blend. Bake at 350° F (175° C) for 30 to 40 minutes or until toothpick inserted in center comes out clean.

Yield: 1 cake

Grapefruit Cake

1 lb.	dates (chopped)	500 g
1 c.	pecans (chopped)	250 mL
3 T.	grapefruit peel (grated)	45 mL
4 c.	all-purpose flour	1 L
1 c.	pure solid shortening	250 mL
2 c.	sugar	500 mL
4	eggs (separated)	4
1 t.	baking soda	5 mL
1½ c.	buttermilk	325 mL
	Grapefruit Cream Frosting (p. 121)	

Combine dates, nuts, and grapefruit peel in bowl; add ¼ c. (60 mL) of the flour. Toss to completely coat; reserve. Cream shortening; gradually add sugar. Continue beating. Beat in egg yolks. Place remaining flour and baking soda in flour sifter. Add alternately with buttermilk to yolk mixture. Fold in reserved date mixture. Beat egg whites until stiff. Fold into batter. Pour into three well-greased and lightly floured 9-in. (23-cm) pans. Bake at 350° F (175° C) for 30 to 35 minutes or until toothpick inserted in center comes out clean. Cool 5 minutes. Remove to cooling racks. Cool completely. Frost with Grapefruit Cream Frosting.

Yield: One 9-in. (23-cm) cake

Cake Mix

2 qt. (8 c.)	all-purpose flour	2 L
1 qt. (4 c.)	cornstarch	1 L
6 c.	sugar	1.5 L
¼ c.	baking powder	60 mL
1 T.	salt	15 mL

Combine all ingredients in large bowl or roaster. Stir to blend. Sift ingredients into 6-qt. (6-L) storage container.

Yield: 5 qt. (5 L)

Yellow Cake

4 c. (1 qt.)	Cake Mix (p. 112)	1000 mL (1 L)
1¼ c.	milk	310 mL
⅓ c.	pure vegetable oil	90 mL
2	eggs	2
1 t.	pure vanilla extract	5 mL

Combine all ingredients in large mixing bowl. Beat until smooth and creamy. Pour into well-greased and lightly floured pans. Bake at 350° F (175° C) until toothpick inserted in center comes out clean.

Two 8-in. (20-cm) round pans	.... 30 to 35 minutes
Two 9-in. (23-cm) round pans	.... 25 to 30 minutes
13 × 9-in. (33 × 23-cm) pan	..... 30 to 35 minutes
24 to 30 cupcakes	.... 20 to 25 minutes

Lemon Cake

4 c. (1 qt.)	Cake Mix (p. 112)	1000 mL (1 L)
¾ c.	milk	190 mL
½ c.	lemon juice	125 mL
⅓ c.	pure vegetable oil	90 mL
2	eggs	2
2 t.	lemon peel (grated)	10 mL

Combine all ingredients in large mixing bowl. Beat until smooth and creamy. Pour into well-greased and lightly floured pans. Bake at 350° F (175° C) until toothpick inserted in center comes out clean.

Two 8-in. (20-cm) round pans .... 30 to 35 minutes
Two 9-in. (23-cm) round pans .... 25 to 30 minutes
13 × 9-in. (33 × 23-cm) pan ..... 30 to 35 minutes
24 to 30 cupcakes .... 20 to 25 minutes

White Cake

4 c. (1 qt.)	Cake Mix (p. 112)	1000 mL (1 L)
1¼ c.	milk	310 mL
⅓ c.	pure vegetable oil	90 mL
2	egg whites	2
1 t.	pure vanilla extract	5 mL

Combine all ingredients in large mixing bowl. Beat until smooth and creamy. Pour into well-greased and lightly floured pans. Bake at 350° F (175° C) until toothpick inserted in center comes out clean.

Two 8-in. (20-cm) round pans .... 30 to 35 minutes
Two 9-in. (23-cm) round pans .... 25 to 30 minutes
13 × 9-in. (33 × 23-cm) pan ..... 30 to 35 minutes
24 to 30 cupcakes .... 20 to 25 minutes

Lazy Day Cake

1 c.	all-purpose flour	250 mL
¾ c.	sugar	190 mL
1	banana (mashed)	1
½ c.	pineapple (crushed)	125 mL
1 c.	pecans (broken)	250 mL
2	eggs	2
½ c.	pure vegetable oil	125 mL
½ t. each	salt, baking soda, cinnamon, pure vanilla extract	2 mL each

Combine all ingredients in ungreased 9 × 9-in. (23 × 23-cm) pan. Stir to blend. Bake at 350° F (175° C) for 30 to 40 minutes or until toothpick inserted in center comes out clean.

Yield: 1 cake

Chocolate Cake

4 c. (1 qt.)	Cake Mix (p. 112)	1000 mL (1 L)
1½ c.	milk	375 mL
½ c.	pure cocoa	125 mL
⅓ c.	pure vegetable oil	90 mL
2	eggs	2
1 t.	pure vanilla extract	5 mL

Combine all ingredients in large mixing bowl. Beat until smooth and creamy. Pour into well-greased and lightly floured pans. Bake at 350° F (175° C) until toothpick inserted in center comes out clean.

Two 8-in. (20-cm) round pans .... 30 to 35 minutes
Two 9-in. (23-cm) round pans .... 25 to 30 minutes
13 × 9-in. (33 × 23-cm) pan   ..... 30 to 35 minutes
24 to 30 cupcakes .... 20 to 25 minutes

Date Snack Cake

½ c.	dates (chopped)	125 mL
½ t.	salt	2 mL
¼ t.	baking soda	1 mL
¾ c.	water (boiling)	190 mL
½ c.	pure solid shortening	125 mL
¼ c.	sugar	60 mL
¼ c.	honey	60 mL
1	egg	1
1 c.	all-purpose flour	250 mL
1 T.	pure cocoa	15 mL
1 t.	pure vanilla extract	5 mL

Combine dates, salt, and baking soda in mixing bowl. Add boiling water. Cover; set aside. Cream shortening. Add remaining ingredients and date mixture. Stir to blend thoroughly. Pour into well-greased and lightly floured 9 × 5-in. (23 × 13-cm) pan. Bake at 350° F (175° C) for 30 minutes, or until done.

Yield: 1 snack cake

White Cake Roll

4	eggs	4
1 c.	sugar	250 mL
¼ c.	water	60 mL
1 t.	pure vanilla extract	5 mL
1 c.	cake flour	250 mL
1 t.	baking powder	5 mL
dash	salt	dash

Beat eggs until lemon-colored. Beat in sugar, water, and vanilla extract. Place cake flour, baking powder, and salt in flour sifter. Sift ⅓ of flour mixture over eggs. Beat thoroughly. Repeat twice more. Pour into 15 × 10-in. (39 × 25-cm) jelly-roll pan which has been lined with waxed paper, greased, and lightly floured. Spread evenly. Bake at 400° F (200° C) for 10 to 12 minutes or until toothpick inserted in center comes out clean. Turn out onto towel sprinkled with confectioners' sugar. Remove waxed paper; cut away dry edges of cake. Roll up towel and cake, jelly-roll style. Cool completely. Unroll; spread with favorite filling. Reroll.

Yield: 1 cake

Pink Cake

4 c. (1 qt.)	Cake Mix (p. 112)	1000 mL (1 L)
¾ c.	milk	190 mL
½ c.	cranberry juice or homemade food coloring (p. 20)	125 mL
⅓ c.	pure vegetable oil	90 mL
2	egg whites	2

Combine ingredients in large mixing bowl. Beat until smooth and creamy. Pour into well-greased and lightly floured pans. Bake at 350° F (175° C) until toothpick inserted in center comes out clean.

Two 8-in. (20-cm) round pans .... 30 to 35 minutes
Two 9-in. (23-cm) round pans .... 25 to 30 minutes
13 × 9-in. (33 × 23-cm) pan ..... 30 to 35 minutes
24 to 30 cupcakes .... 20 to 25 minutes

Crazy Cake

1½ c.	all-purpose flour	375 mL
1 c.	sugar	250 mL
1 c.	water (cold)	250 mL
⅓ c.	pure vegetable oil	90 mL
¼ c.	pure cocoa	60 mL
1 T.	distilled white vinegar	15 mL
1 t.	pure vanilla extract	5 mL
1 t.	baking soda	5 mL
½ t.	salt	2 mL

Combine all ingredients in ungreased 8 × 8-in. (20 × 20-cm) pan. Stir to blend. Bake at 350° F (175° C) for 30 to 35 minutes or until toothpick inserted in center comes out clean.

Yield: 1 cake

Rhubarb Dump Cake

1 c.	milk	250 mL
1 t.	lemon juice	5 mL
1½ c.	brown sugar (packed)	375 mL
½ c.	sweet butter (melted)	125 mL
2 c.	flour	500 mL
1½ c.	rhubarb (cut fine)	375 mL
1	egg	1
1 t.	baking soda	5 mL
¼ t.	salt	1 mL
¼ c.	sugar	60 mL
1 t.	cinnamon	5 mL

Mix milk and lemon juice in bowl. Allow to sour 5 minutes. Add remaining ingredients, except ¼ c. (60 mL) sugar and the cinnamon. Stir to blend. Pour into 9 × 13-in. (33 × 23-cm) baking dish. Sprinkle with the sugar and cinnamon. Bake at 350° F (175° C) for 30 to 35 minutes or until done.

Microwave: Cook on Low 9 minutes. Increase heat to High and cook 6 to 7 minutes or until toothpick inserted in center comes out clean.

Yield: 1 cake

Sponge Cake

9	egg yolks	9
1½ c.	sugar	325 mL
¾ c.	water (boiling)	190 mL
2¼ c.	all-purpose flour (sifted)	560 mL
½ t.	salt	2 mL
1 T.	baking powder	15 mL
2 t.	pure vanilla extract	10 mL

Beat egg yolks until light and fluffy; gradually add sugar. Continue beating; add boiling water. Fold flour, salt, and baking powder into yolk mixture. Add vanilla extract. Pour into ungreased 9-in. (23-cm) tube pan with removable bottom. Bake at 350° F (175° C) for 45 to 50 minutes. Invert until cool. Remove cake from pan and trim off any hard edges. Frost, or sprinkle with confectioners' sugar.

Yield: One 9-in. (23-cm) tube cake

Angel Food Cake

9	egg whites (at room temperature)	9
1 t.	cream of tartar	5 mL
1 t.	pure vanilla extract	5 mL
1 c.	sugar	250 mL
1 c.	cake flour (sifted)	250 mL
1 t.	salt	5 mL

Whip egg whites to soft peaks; add cream of tartar. Whip until very stiff. Fold in vanilla extract. Combine sugar, sifted flour, and salt in flour sifter. Sift ¼ of sugar mixture over egg whites. Fold completely into egg whites. Repeat three more times. Pour into ungreased 9-in. (23-cm) tube pan with removable bottom. Bake at 350° F (175° C) for 45 to 50 minutes or until done. Invert until cool. Remove cake from pan and trim off any hard edges.

Yield: One 9-in. (23-cm) tube cake

Coconut Cake

¾ c.	sweet butter	190 mL
3	eggs (separated)	3
3 c.	Cake Mix (p. 112)	750 mL
¾ c.	pure coconut milk	190 mL
½ t.	pure vanilla extract	2 mL
1 c.	unsweetened coconut (grated)	250 mL
	pure favorite jelly	
	Quick White Frosting (p. 122)	

Cream butter until light and fluffy. Beat in egg yolks, one at a time. Add Cake Mix alternately with coconut milk and vanilla extract until smooth. Stir in grated coconut. Beat egg whites until stiff; fold into batter. Pour into two well-greased and lightly floured 9-in. (23-cm) pans. Bake at 350° F (175° C) for 25 to 30 minutes or until toothpick inserted in center comes out clean. Cool 5 minutes; remove to cooling rack. When completely cool, fill cake layers with favorite jelly. Frost with Quick White Frosting; sprinkle with extra coconut.

Yield: One 9-in. (23-cm) cake

Marble Cake

1 recipe	White Cake (p. 113)	1 recipe
½ c.	pure cocoa	125 mL
1 t.	cinnamon	5 mL
¼ t.	salt	1 mL
pinch	baking soda	pinch

Prepare White Cake batter; divide between two bowls. Stir cocoa, cinnamon, salt, and baking soda thoroughly into batter in one of the bowls. Grease and lightly flour 9-in. (23-cm) tube pan or bundt pan. Fill with cake batter, alternating large spoonfuls of white and chocolate batter. Bake at 350° F (175° C) for 50 to 60 minutes or until toothpick inserted in cake comes out clean. Cool 5 minutes; remove to rack.

Yield: One 9-in. (23-cm) cake

Banana–Poppy Seed Snack Cake

¼ c.	poppy seeds	60 mL
¾ c.	milk	190 mL
3 c.	Cake Mix (p. 112)	750 mL
½ c.	banana (mashed)	125 mL
⅓ c.	pure vegetable oil	90 mL
2	eggs	2
1 t.	pure vanilla extract	5 mL

Combine poppy seeds and milk. Allow to rest 5 minutes. Combine remaining ingredients in mixing bowl. Add the milk mixture. Beat until smooth and creamy. Pour into well-greased and lightly floured 8-in. (20-cm) square pan. Bake at 350° F (175° C) for 30 to 40 minutes or until toothpick inserted in center comes out clean.

Yield: 1 snack cake

Pear-Walnut Snack Cake

3 c.	Cake Mix (p. 112)	750 mL
½ c.	milk	125 mL
7-oz. jar	toddler junior pears	213-g jar
⅓ c.	pure vegetable oil	90 mL
2	eggs	2
1 t.	pure vanilla extract	5 mL
¼ c.	walnuts (chopped)	60 mL

Combine all ingredients (except walnuts) in mixing bowl. Beat until smooth and creamy. Stir in walnuts. Pour into a well-greased and lightly floured 8-in. (20-cm) square pan. Bake at 350° F (175° C) for 30 to 40 minutes or until toothpick inserted in center comes out clean.

Yield: 1 snack cake

FROSTINGS AND FILLINGS

Chocolate Frosting

1 c.	sugar	250 mL
¼ c.	pure cocoa	60 mL
¼ c.	sweet butter	60 mL
¼ c.	milk	60 mL
dash	salt	dash
1 t.	pure vanilla extract	5 mL

Combine all ingredients except vanilla extract in saucepan. Cook and stir over medium heat until mixture comes to boil; cook 1 minute. Remove from heat; stir in vanilla extract. Cool completely. Beat to fluff.

Yield: 2 c. (500 mL)

Peanut Butter Frosting

1 c.	pure peanut butter	250 mL
1 c.	pure evaporated milk	250 mL
½ c.	brown sugar (packed)	125 mL

Combine all ingredients in saucepan. Cook and stir over medium heat until mixture comes to a boil. Boil 5 minutes. Cool. Beat well.

Yield: 2 c. (500 mL)

Grapefruit Cream Frosting

½ c.	sweet butter	125 mL
1 T.	flour	15 mL
½ t.	salt	2 mL
½ c.	grapefruit juice	125 mL
¼ c.	grapefruit peel (grated)	60 mL
3½ c.	confectioners' sugar	875 mL

Soften butter; cream with flour and salt. Add grapefruit juice and peel. Beat in confectioners' sugar until smooth.

Yield: 2 c. (500 mL)

Custard Frosting

½ c.	sugar	125 mL
2 T.	cornstarch	30 mL
2	egg yolks	2
1 c.	milk	250 mL
½ c.	pure solid shortening	125 mL
2 T.	sweet butter	30 mL
⅓ c.	confectioners' sugar	90 mL

Combine sugar, cornstarch, egg yolks, and milk in saucepan. Cook and stir over low heat until thickened. Cool completely. Cream shortening and butter; add confectioners' sugar. Beat until smooth; gradually beat in cool custard. Beat thoroughly.

Yield: 2 c. (500 mL)

Mango Fluff Topping

1 c.	mango (puréed)	250 mL
½ c.	honey	125 mL
1	egg white	1

Combine all ingredients in mixing bowl. Beat until light and fluffy. Use to top ice cream, pies, or cakes.

Yield: 1½ c. (325 mL)

Quick White Frosting

1	egg white	1
1 t.	pure vanilla extract	5 mL
¼ t.	cream of tartar	1 mL
¾ c.	sugar	190 mL
¼ c.	water (boiling)	60 mL

Combine egg white, vanilla extract, cream of tartar, and sugar in deep narrow bowl. Stir to mix. Beat in boiling water. Continue beating to stiff peaks.

Yield: 2 c. (500 mL)

Doughnut Glaze

1½ c.	confectioners' sugar	325 mL
2 t.	light corn syrup	10 mL
½ t.	pure vanilla extract	2 mL
3 T.	water (boiling)	45 mL

Combine all ingredients; mix thoroughly. Dip or brush on cooled doughnuts.

Yield: ½ c. (125 mL)

Banana Spread

2	bananas (very ripe)	2
¾ c.	sugar	190 mL
1	egg white	1
dash	salt	dash

Combine ingredients. Beat until thick and fluffy.

Yield: 4 to 5 c. (1000 to 1250 mL)

Vanilla Cookie Filling

3 c.	confectioners' sugar	750 mL
5 T.	sweet butter	65 mL
1 t.	pure vanilla extract	5 mL
¼ t.	salt	1 mL
3 to 4 T.	light cream or milk	45 to 60 mL

Combine ingredients in mixing bowl. Stir or whip until fluffy and thick enough to spread.

Yield: 1½ c. (375 mL)

Chocolate Cookie Filling

2 c.	confectioners' sugar	500mL
½ c.	pure cocoa	125 mL
1 T.	sweet butter (melted)	15 mL
1 t.	pure vanilla extract	5 mL
2 to 3 T.	milk (hot)	30 to 45 mL

Mix sugar and cocoa in mixing bowl. Add melted butter, vanilla extract, and hot milk. Stir or whip until fluffy and thick enough to spread.

Yield: 1¼ c. (310 mL)

Lemon Filling

1½ c.	water	375 mL
½ c.	sugar	125 mL
½ c.	lemon juice	125 mL
1	egg	1
3 T.	cornstarch	45 mL
2 t.	lemon peel (grated)	10 mL
dash	salt	dash

Combine all ingredients in a saucepan. Bring to boil; reduce heat. Stir and cook until thickened.

Yield: 2 c. (500 mL)

Milk Chocolate Filling

1½ c.	milk	375 mL
1 c.	sugar	250 mL
½ c.	water	125 mL
¼ c.	pure cocoa	60 mL
2	eggs (beaten)	2
3 T.	cornstarch	45 mL
dash	salt	dash
1 t.	pure vanilla extract	5 mL

Combine all ingredients except vanilla extract in a saucepan. Bring to a boil; reduce heat. Stir and cook until thickened. Remove from heat. Stir in vanilla extract.

Yield: 2 c. (500 mL)

Pineapple Filling

1½ c.	crushed pineapple (with juice)	375 mL
½ c.	water	125 mL
½ c.	sugar	125 mL
1	egg (beaten)	1
1 T.	cornstarch	15 mL

Combine all ingredients in a saucepan; bring to boil. Reduce heat; stir and cook until thickened.

Yield: 2 c. (500 mL)

Pudding Mix

2 qt.	sugar	2 L
1 c.	flour	250 mL
1 c.	cornstarch	250 mL
1 t.	salt	5 mL

Combine ingredients in large pan or bowl. Stir to mix thoroughly. Sift mixture three times. Store in covered container.

Yield: 2½ qt. (2.5 L)

Chocolate Fudge Pudding and Pie Filling

1 c.	Pudding Mix (p. 124)	250 mL
2 c.	water	500 mL
3 T.	pure cocoa	45 mL
½ t.	pure vanilla extract	2 mL
1 T.	sweet butter	15 mL

Combine Pudding Mix, water, and cocoa in saucepan. Cook and stir over medium heat until mixture comes to a boil. Reduce heat; cook and stir for 2 to 3 minutes or until desired thickness. Remove from heat. Stir in vanilla extract and butter.

Microwave: Combine mix, water, and cocoa in large bowl. Cook on High for 4 minutes. Stir. Reduce heat to Medium; cook for 3 to 4 minutes or until desired thickness. Stir in vanilla extract and butter.

Yield: 2 c. (500 mL)

Lemon Pudding and Pie Filling

1 c.	Pudding Mix (p. 124)	250 mL
1½ c.	water	325 mL
½ c.	lemon juice	125 mL
2 t.	lemon peel (grated)	10 mL
1 T.	sweet butter	15 mL

Combine Pudding Mix, water, and lemon juice in saucepan. Cook and stir over medium heat until mixture comes to a boil. Reduce heat. Cook and stir for 2 to 3 minutes or until desired thickness. Remove from heat; stir in lemon peel and butter.

Microwave: Combine mix, water, and lemon juice in large bowl. Cook on High for 4 minutes. Stir. Reduce heat. Cook on Medium for 3 to 4 minutes or until desired thickness. Stir in lemon peel and butter.

Yield: 2 c. (500 mL)

French Vanilla Pudding and Pie Filling

1 c.	Pudding Mix (p. 124)	250 mL
2 c.	milk	500 mL
2	egg yolks (slightly beaten)	2
½ t.	pure vanilla extract	2 mL
1 T.	sweet butter	15 mL

Combine Pudding Mix and milk in saucepan. Cook and stir over medium heat until mixture comes to a boil. Pour small amount of pudding into egg yolks; stir to blend. Pour egg yolks into pudding mixture. Return to heat. Stir and cook over low heat 2 to 3 minutes. DO NOT BOIL. Remove from heat. Stir in vanilla extract and butter. (Pudding thickens as it cools.)

Microwave: Combine mix and milk in large bowl. Cook on High for 4 minutes. Stir; pour small amount of pudding into egg yolks. Pour egg yolks into pudding mixture. Return to microwave. Cook on Medium for 3 to 4 minutes. Stir in vanilla extract and butter.

Yield: 2 c. (500 mL)

Milk Chocolate Pudding and Pie Filling

1 c.	Pudding Mix (p. 124)	250 mL
2 c.	milk	500 mL
½ c.	pure cocoa	125 mL
½ t.	pure vanilla extract	2 mL
1 T.	sweet butter	15 mL

Combine Pudding Mix, milk, and cocoa in saucepan. Cook and stir over medium heat until mixture comes to a boil. Reduce heat; cook and stir for 2 to 3 minutes or until desired thickness. Remove from heat; stir in vanilla extract and butter.

Microwave: Combine mix, milk, and cocoa in large bowl. Cook on High for 4 minutes. Stir. Reduce heat to Medium and cook for 3 to 4 minutes or until desired thickness. Stir in vanilla extract and butter.

Yield: 2 c. (500 mL)

Coconut Cream Pudding and Pie Filling

1 c.	Pudding Mix (p. 124)	250 mL
2 c.	milk	500 mL
1 c.	unsweetened coconut (grated)	250 mL
½ t.	pure vanilla extract	2 mL
1 T.	sweet butter	15 mL

Combine Pudding Mix and milk in saucepan. Cook and stir over medium heat until mixture comes to a boil; reduce heat. Cook and stir 2 to 3 minutes or until desired thickness. Remove from heat. Stir in coconut, vanilla extract, and butter.

Microwave: Combine mix and milk in large bowl. Cook on High for 4 minutes. Stir. Reduce heat to Medium and cook for 3 to 4 minutes or until desired thickness. Stir in coconut, vanilla extract, and butter.

Yield: 2 c. (500 mL)

Banana Cream Pudding and Pie Filling

1 c.	Pudding Mix (p. 124)	250 mL
2 c.	milk	500 mL
2	bananas (mashed)	2
½ t.	pure vanilla extract	2 mL
1 T.	sweet butter	15 mL

Combine Pudding Mix and milk in saucepan. Cook and stir over medium heat until mixture comes to a boil. Reduce heat. Cook and stir 2 to 3 minutes or until desired thickness. Remove from heat. Stir in bananas, vanilla extract, and butter.

Microwave: Combine mix and milk in large bowl. Cook on High for 4 minutes. Stir. Reduce heat to Medium and cook for 3 to 4 minutes or until desired thickness. Stir in bananas, vanilla extract, and butter.

Yield: 2 c. (500 mL)

COOKIES

Double Date Bars

Pastry:

2½ c.	all-purpose flour	625 mL
⅔ c.	sugar	160 mL
½ c.	sweet butter	125 mL
½ c.	pure solid shortening	125 mL

Combine all ingredients. With food processor or pastry blender, mix until the texture of cornmeal. Pack into 14 × 10-in. (35 × 25-cm) pan. Bake at 350° F (175° C) for 20 minutes. Remove from oven.

Date Layer:

1 c.	brown sugar (packed)	250 mL
⅓ c.	sugar	90 mL
4	eggs	4
2 t.	pure vanilla extract	10 mL
¼ c.	all-purpose flour	60 mL
2 t.	baking powder	10 mL
½ t.	nutmeg	2 mL
½ t.	salt	2 mL
1 lb.	dates (cut up)	500 g
2 c.	walnuts (chopped)	500 mL

Combine sugars, eggs, and vanilla extract. Beat until smooth. Stir in flour, baking powder, nutmeg, and salt. Fold in dates and nuts. Pour over baked pastry. Bake at 350° F (175° C) for 20 minutes or until set. If desired, sprinkle with confectioners' sugar.

Yield: Thirty-five 2-in. (5-cm) bars

Chinese Chews

1¼ c.	sugar	310 mL
¾ c.	all-purpose flour	190 mL
1 t.	baking powder	5 mL
1 c.	walnuts (powdered)	250 mL
1 c.	dates (finely chopped)	250 mL
¼ c.	water	60 mL

Sift sugar, flour, and baking powder into mixing bowl. Add nuts and dates. Stir in water to make a smooth soft dough. Spread out thinly on a well-greased and chilled 14 × 10-in. (35 × 25-cm) cooking tin. Bake at 325° F (165° C) for 10 to 12 minutes. Cut into squares. Carefully remove each square and roll around handle of wooden spoon. (If cookie becomes cool before rolling, place back in oven for 1 to 2 seconds.) Store at least a week before serving.

Yield: 30 cookies

Vanilla Sandwich Cookies

½ c.	pure solid shortening	125 mL
1 c.	sugar	250 mL
1	egg	1
1 t.	pure vanilla extract	5 mL
1½ t.	baking soda	7 mL
½ t.	salt	2 mL
3 T.	light cream or milk	45 mL
2⅔ c.	all-purpose flour (sifted)	680 mL
1 recipe	Vanilla or Chocolate Cookie Filling (p. 123)	1 recipe

Cream together the shortening and sugar; beat in egg and vanilla extract. Add baking soda, salt, and light cream or milk. Stir to blend. Work in flour. Cover and chill thoroughly. Roll dough, a third at a time, to ⅛-in. (8-mm) thickness on lightly floured board. Cut into 1-in. (2.5-cm) rounds. Place on ungreased cookie sheet. Bake at 400° F (200° C) for 8 to 10 minutes or until done. Cool on racks. Spread one cookie with Vanilla or Chocolate Cookie Filling; top with second cookie.

Yield: 3 to 3½ dozen filled cookies

Marie's Pecan Fingers

1 c.	sweet butter	250 mL
½ c.	confectioners' sugar	125 mL
2 c.	all-purpose flour	500 mL
½ t.	salt	2 mL
2 t.	pure vanilla extract	10 mL
1 T.	water	15 mL
2 c.	pecans (chopped fine)	500 mL

Cream the butter. Add confectioners' sugar, 1 T. (15 mL) at a time. Beat until smooth. Gradually add 1 c. (250 mL) of the flour and the salt. Beat well after each addition. Beat in vanilla extract and water. Add remaining flour and pecans. Roll in palms of hands to form fingers. Place on 14 × 10-in. (35 × 25-cm) cookie tin. Bake at 375° F (190° C) for 12 to 15 minutes. Roll in extra confectioners' sugar while warm.

Yield: 2 to 3 dozen cookies

Banana Bars

2½ c.	all-purpose flour	625 mL
2 c.	sugar	500 mL
1½ t.	baking powder	7 mL
1 t.	baking soda	5 mL
½ t.	salt	2 mL
¾ c.	pure solid shortening	190 mL
⅔ c.	buttermilk	160 mL
1¼ c.	banana (mashed)	310 mL
2	eggs	2

Combine all ingredients in mixing bowl. Stir until well blended. Pour into waxed paper-lined 15 × 10-in. (39 × 25-cm) jelly-roll pan. Bake at 350° F (175° C) for 30 to 40 minutes or until toothpick inserted in center comes out clean. Remove from oven; cool slightly. Flip over onto towel; remove waxed paper. Cool; cut into bars. Frost if desired.

Yield: 25 bars

Pecan Bars

¾ c.	pure vegetable oil	190 mL
1 c.	brown sugar (packed)	250 mL
1 c.	sugar	250 mL
2	eggs	2
1¼ c.	all-purpose flour	310 mL
½ t.	baking soda	2 mL
1 t.	pure vanilla extract	5 mL
1 c.	pecans (chopped)	250 mL

Combine oil, sugars, and eggs; beat well. Blend in flour, baking soda, vanilla extract, and pecans. Pour into lightly greased 14 × 10-in. (35 × 25-cm) cookie sheet. Bake at 350° F (175° C) for 30 to 40 minutes or until set. Remove from oven; cool until slightly warm. Cut into bars.

Yield: 20 to 24 bars

Erio Cookies

¾ c.	pure solid shortening	190 mL
1 c.	sugar	250 mL
1	egg	1
½ t.	pure vanilla extract	2 mL
2 c.	all-purpose flour (sifted)	500 mL
1 t.	baking powder	5 mL
½ t.	salt	2 mL
⅔ c.	pure cocoa	160 mL
¼ c.	milk	60 mL
1 recipe	Vanilla Cookie Filling (p. 123)	1 recipe

Cream together the shortening and sugar; beat in egg and vanilla extract. Add dry ingredients and milk alternately to creamed mixture. Cover and chill thoroughly. Roll dough, a third at a time, to ⅛-in. (8-mm) thickness on lightly floured board. Cut into 1-in. (2.5-cm) rounds. Place on ungreased cookie sheets. Bake at 400° F (200° C) for 8 to 10 minutes or until done. Cool on racks. Spread one cookie with Vanilla Cookie Filling. Top with second cookie.

Yield: 3 to 3½ dozen filled cookies

Old World Sugar Cookies

1 c.	sweet butter	250 mL
1 c.	pure vegetable oil	250 mL
1 c.	confectioners' sugar	250 mL
1 c.	sugar	250 mL
2	eggs	2
2 t.	pure vanilla extract	10 mL
5 c.	all-purpose flour	1250 mL
1 t.	salt	5 mL
1 t.	baking soda	5 mL
1 t.	cream of tartar	5 mL

Cream together butter, oil, and sugars until light and fluffy. Beat in eggs and vanilla extract. Sift dry ingredients together. Add to creamed mixture and stir thoroughly. Roll into 1 to 1½-in. (3 to 4-cm) balls. Place on ungreased cookie sheet. Press with sugar-dipped glass. Bake at 350° F (175° C) for 15 to 20 minutes.

Yield: 5 to 6 dozen cookies

Hickory Nut Cookies

1 c.	pure solid shortening	250 mL
½ c.	sugar	125 mL
½ c.	brown sugar (packed)	125 mL
2	eggs	2
2 t.	pure vanilla extract	10 mL
2½ c.	flour	625 mL
½ t.	baking soda	2 mL
1½ t.	salt	7 mL
1 c.	hickory nuts (chopped fine)	250 mL

Cream together shortening, sugars, eggs, and vanilla extract. Add remaining ingredients; mix thoroughly. Divide dough in half. Roll each half into a log, 1 to 1½ in. (3 to 4 cm) in diameter. Wrap in plastic wrap or waxed paper. Chill overnight. Cut into thin ⅛-in. (4-mm) slices. Place on ungreased cookie sheets. Bake at 350° F (175° C) for 6 to 8 minutes.

Yield: 6 dozen cookies

Pineapple Cookies

4 c.	all-purpose flour	1000 mL
1 c.	pure solid shortening	250 mL
1 c.	sugar	250 mL
1 c.	brown sugar (packed)	250 mL
1 c.	crushed pineapple	250 mL
2	eggs (beaten)	2
1 t.	pure vanilla extract	5 mL
1 t.	baking soda	5 mL

Combine ingredients in large mixing bowl. Stir to blend. Drop by spoonfuls onto lightly greased cookie sheet. Bake at 350° F (175° C) for 12 to 15 minutes.

Yield: 5 dozen cookies

Pecan Butter Squares

¾ c.	sweet butter	190 mL
3 T.	sugar	45 mL
½ c.	flour	125 mL
3	egg yolks (well beaten)	3
2½ c.	brown sugar (packed)	625 mL
1 c.	pecans (chopped)	250 mL
1 c.	pure coconut (shredded)	250 mL
3	egg whites (stiffly beaten)	3
	confectioners' sugar	

Cream together butter and sugar; blend in flour. Pour into well-greased 13 × 9-in. (33 × 23-cm) pan. Bake at 375° F (190° C) for 15 minutes. (Do not turn off oven.) Beat egg yolks with brown sugar; add pecans and coconut. Fold into stiffly beaten egg whites. Pour pecan mixture over butter crust; spread evenly. Return to 375° F (190° C) oven. Bake 25 to 30 minutes or until completely set. Cool slightly. Dust with confectioners' sugar. Cut into 1½-in. (4-cm) squares.

Yield: 24 squares

Cinnamon Sticks

1 c.	pure solid shortening	250 mL
½ c.	sugar	125 mL
½ c.	brown sugar (packed)	125 mL
2	eggs	2
1 t.	pure vanilla extract	5 mL
2¾ c.	all-purpose flour	690 mL
½ t.	baking soda	2 mL
1 t.	salt	5 mL
2 t.·	cinnamon	10 mL
1 t.	nutmeg	5 mL
	additional sugar	

Cream together shortening, sugars, eggs, and vanilla extract. Add remaining ingredients (except additional sugar). Mix thoroughly. Chill thoroughly or overnight. Form into finger-length sticks. Roll in sugar. Place on ungreased cookie sheet. Bake at 350° F (175° C) for 8 to 10 minutes.

Yield: 5½ to 6 dozen sticks

Black Walnut Form Cookies

3½ c.	all-purpose flour	825 mL
2 c.	sugar	500 mL
1 t.	baking powder	5 mL
1 c.	pure solid shortening	250 mL
1 c.	sweet butter	250 mL
1	egg (beaten)	1
2 t.	pure vanilla extract	10 mL
¼ c.	black walnuts (chopped fine)	60 mL

Combine all ingredients. Mix thoroughly with hands until dough is smooth. Roll out on lightly floured board to ¼-in. (8-mm) thickness. Cut into desired shapes. Place on ungreased cookie sheets. Bake at 375° F (190° C) for 10 to 12 minutes or until lightly browned.

Yield: 4 to 5 dozen cookies

Soft Molasses Cookies

¼ c.	pure solid shortening	60 mL
¼ c.	brown sugar	60 mL
¼ c.	sour milk (hot)	60 mL
2 t.	distilled white vinegar	10 mL
¼ c.	unsulphured molasses	60 mL
1	egg (beaten)	1
1½ c.	all-purpose flour	375 mL
1 t.	baking powder	5 mL
1 t.	cinnamon	5 mL
¼ t.	ginger	1 mL
½ c.	dates (floured and cut)	125 mL

Cream shortening with brown sugar. Add sour milk, vinegar, molasses, and egg. Beat well. Add dry ingredients and dates. Stir to blend thoroughly. Drop by spoonfuls onto greased cookie sheet. Bake at 350° F (175° C) for 15 minutes.

Yield: 3 to 4 dozen cookies

Bitter Chocolate Cookies

4	egg whites	4
1 c.	sugar	250 mL
1 t.	pure vanilla extract	5 mL
3 squares (1 oz. each)	pure bitter chocolate (grated)	3 squares (30 g each)
1½ c.	walnuts (chopped)	375 mL

Beat egg whites to soft peaks. Gradually add sugar, beating until stiff. Beat in vanilla extract. Fold in grated bitter chocolate and nuts. Drop onto cookie sheets lined with brown paper. Bake at 350° F (175° C) for 20 to 25 minutes (watch carefully). To remove cookies from brown paper, place the hot paper on wet towel. Remove cookies carefully.

Yield: 4 to 5 dozen cookies

Double Bubble Squares

Pastry:

2½ c.	all-purpose flour	625 mL
⅔ c.	sugar	160 mL
1 c.	pure solid shortening	250 mL
1 t.	salt	5 mL

Blend all ingredients together thoroughly. Pack into 14 × 10-in. (35 × 25-cm) cookie or jelly-roll sheet. Bake at 350° F (175° C) for 20 minutes or until edges are lightly browned.

Top Layer:

⅔ c.	brown sugar (packed)	160 mL
⅔ c.	sugar	160 mL
4	eggs	4
2 t.	pure vanilla extract	10 mL
¼ c.	all-purpose flour	60 mL
2 t.	baking powder	10 mL
½ t.	nutmeg	2 mL
½ t.	salt	2 mL
2 c.	walnuts (chopped)	500 mL
2 c.	dates (floured and cut)	500 mL

Beat sugars, eggs, and vanilla extract until well blended. Add flour, baking powder, nutmeg, and salt. Beat until smooth. Stir in walnuts and dates. Pour evenly over pastry crust. Bake at 350° F (175° C) for 20 to 25 minutes or until set. Cool. Cut into squares or sticks.

Yield: 35 to 40 squares

Date Melt-a-Ways

3	egg whites	3
1 c.	sugar	250 mL
1 c.	dates (floured and cut fine)	250 mL
1 c.	pecans or walnuts (chopped)	250 mL
½ t.	pure vanilla extract	2 mL

Beat egg whites until very stiff. Slowly add sugar, beating constantly. Stir in remaining ingredients. Drop onto cookie sheets lined with waxed paper. Bake at 325° F (165° C) for 8 to 10 minutes or until lightly browned. Remove carefully onto cookie racks.

Yield: 45 to 60 cookies

Butternut Cookies

½ c.	sweet butter	125 mL
1 c.	brown sugar (packed)	250 mL
1	egg	1
1 c.	flour	250 mL
½ c.	butternuts (broken)	125 mL
1 t.	pure vanilla extract	5 mL

Cream together butter and brown sugar. Add remaining ingredients. Drop onto lightly greased cookie sheet. Bake at 350° F (175° C) for 10 to 12 minutes.

Yield: 20 to 24 cookies

Refrigerator Chocolate Cookies

½ c.	pure solid shortening	125 mL
¾ c.	brown sugar (packed)	190 mL
1	egg	1
3 T.	pure cocoa	45 mL
1 t.	pure vanilla extract	5 mL
1¾ c.	all-purpose flour	440 mL
½ t.	baking soda	2 mL
½ t.	salt	2 mL

Cream shortening and brown sugar until fluffy. Beat in egg, cocoa, and vanilla extract. Add flour, baking soda, and salt. Shape into two logs, 2 in. (5 cm) in diameter. Wrap tightly in plastic wrap or waxed paper. Secure ends. Refrigerate. When ready to bake, cut into ⅛ in. (3-mm) slices. Place on greased cookie sheets. Bake at 350° F (175° C) for 10 to 12 minutes.

Yield: 5 to 5½ dozen cookies

PIES AND PASTRIES

Perky Pear Pie

Filling:

9-in.	pie pastry (unbaked)	23-cm
8	pears (hard)	8
1 c.	sugar	250 mL
⅓ c.	brown sugar	90 mL
¼ c.	flour	60 mL
1 t.	cinnamon	5 mL
dash	salt	dash

Prepare pastry for one 9-in. (23-cm) pie shell; line pan. Peel, core, and thinly slice the pears. Combine sugars, flour, cinnamon, and salt; mix with pears. Pile into prepared pie shell.

Topping:

9-in.	pie pastry (unbaked)	23-cm
¼ c.	sugar	60 mL
¼ c.	brown sugar	60 mL
¼ t.	cinnamon	1 mL
¼ t.	nutmeg	1 mL
⅓ c.	walnuts (broken)	90 mL
½ c.	white Cheddar cheese (grated)	125 mL

Combine unrolled pie pastry with sugars, cinnamon, and nutmeg until crumbly. Add walnut pieces; mix in thoroughly. Sprinkle over top of pears. Bake at 400° F (200° C) for 35 minutes. Top with grated cheese. Return to oven for 5 minutes or until cheese melts.

Yield: 1 pie (8 to 10 servings)

Hazelnut Pie

9-in.	pie shell (unbaked)	23-cm
6	eggs	6
2 c.	corn syrup	500 mL
1 c.	sugar	250 mL
½ c.	brown sugar (packed)	125 mL
1 t.	pure vanilla extract	5 mL
¼ t.	salt	1 mL
3 c.	hazelnuts (chopped)	750 mL

Prepare pie shell (do not bake). Beat eggs until lemon-colored. Add corn syrup, sugars, vanilla extract, and salt. Beat until smooth. Stir in hazelnuts. Pour into pie shell. Bake at 350° F (175° C) for 50 to 60 minutes or until set.

Yield: One 9-in. (23-cm) pie

Date Crumb Pie

9-in.	pie shell (unbaked)	23-cm
2 c.	water	500 mL
1 c.	dates (cut up)	250 mL
⅔ c.	brown sugar (packed)	160 mL
1 T.	distilled white vinegar	15 mL
½ t.	salt	2 mL
2 T.	cornstarch	30 mL
¼ c.	water (cold)	60 mL
1 recipe	Crumb Topping (p. 105)	1 recipe

Prepare pie shell (do not bake). Combine 2 c. (500 mL) water, the dates, brown sugar, vinegar, and salt in saucepan; heat to boiling. Blend cornstarch and ¼ c. (60 mL) cold water in screwtop jar. Gradually pour cornstarch mixture into date mixture; stir constantly. Cook over medium heat until clear and thickened. Pour into pie shell. Cover with Crumb Topping. Bake at 375° F (190° C) for 30 to 40 minutes or until browned.

Yield: One 9-in. (23-cm) pie

Whipped Grapefruit Pie

9-in.	pie shell (baked and chilled)	23-cm
1 env.	unflavored gelatin	1 env.
1¼ c.	grapefruit juice	310 mL
1 c.	sugar	250 mL
2 T.	all-purposed flour	30 mL
¼ t.	salt	1 mL
1 T.	grapefruit peel (grated)	15 mL
2 T.	lemon juice	30 mL
1 c.	whipped heavy cream (chilled)	250 mL

Prepare, bake and chill pie shell. Soften gelatin in juice in heavy saucepan. Add sugar, flour, and salt; stir to blend. Cook and stir over medium heat until gelatin is dissolved and mixture is thickened. Remove from heat; add grapefruit peel and lemon juice. Chill, stirring occasionally, until mixture is cool. Thoroughly fold into whipped cream. Pour into pie shell. Chill until firm.

Yield: One 9-in. (23-cm) pie

Deep-Dish Pear Pie

8	pears (hard)	8
1½ c.	sugar	375 mL
¼ c.	all-purpose flour	60 mL
1½ t.	cinnamon	7 mL
¼ t.	nutmeg	1 mL
dash	salt	dash
3 T.	sweet butter	45 mL
9-in.	pie crust (unbaked)	23-cm

Peel and core pears; slice thin. Combine sugar, flour, spices, and salt; mix with pears. Pour into 9-in. (23-cm) deep-dish pie pan. Dot with butter. Adjust pie crust over the top. Prick with fork. Bake at 400° F (200° C) for 40 minutes.

Yield: 1 pie (8 to 10 servings)

Graham-Nuts Pie

9-in.	pie shell (unbaked)	23-cm
½ c.	Graham-Nuts Cereal (p. 109)	125 mL
½ c.	water (lukewarm)	125 mL
1 c.	brown sugar	250 mL
½ c.	honey	125 mL
¼ c.	sweet butter	60 mL
dash	salt	dash
3	eggs	3
1 t.	pure vanilla extract	5 mL

Prepare pie shell (do not bake). Soak Graham-Nuts Cereal in luke-warm water until liquid is absorbed. Combine brown sugar, honey, butter, and salt in saucepan. Bring to boil; remove from heat. Beat eggs until frothy; add small amount of brown sugar mixture and blend. Pour eggs into remaining brown sugar mixture; mix well. Stir in Graham-Nuts and vanilla extract. Pour into pie shell. Bake at 375° F (190° C) for 45 to 50 minutes or until center is set.

Microwave: Cook on Low for 25 to 30 minutes or until set.

Yield: One 9-in. (23-cm) pie

Cantaloupe Cream Pie

9-in.	pie shell (baked)	23-cm
1	cantaloupe	1
1 T.	lemon juice	15 mL
1 env.	unflavored gelatin	1 env.
dash	salt	dash
1 c.	whipping cream	250 mL

Prepare and bake pie shell. Peel, seed, and cut cantaloupe into chunks. Purée cantaloupe in blender. Pour purée into saucepan. Add lemon juice, gelatin, and salt. Allow to rest 10 minutes or until gela-tin has softened. Cook over low heat until gelatin is dissolved. Refrigerate until cooled and thickened. Beat whipping cream until stiff. Beat cantaloupe mixture. Gently fold cantaloupe mixture into whipped cream. Pile into pie shell. Chill until firm.

Yield: One 9-in. (23-cm) pie

Pumpkin Chiffon Pie

9-in.	Graham Cracker Pie Shell (p. 108)	23-cm
2 env.	unflavored gelatin	2 env.
2½ c.	pumpkin (cooked and mashed)	625 mL
1⅓ c.	brown sugar (packed)	340 mL
1 c.	milk	250 mL
6	eggs (separated)	6
1 t.	salt	5 mL
1 t.	cinnamon	5 mL
½ t.	nutmeg	2 mL
½ t.	ginger	2 mL
1 c.	sugar	250 mL
	Honey Graham Cracker crumbs (p. 107)	

Prepare Graham Cracker Pie Shell. Combine gelatin, pumpkin, brown sugar, milk, egg yolks, salt, and spices in saucepan. Cook and stir over medium heat until mixture comes to a boil. Remove from heat. Cool. Whip egg whites into soft peaks, gradually adding sugar. Beat until stiff. Fold egg whites into cooled pumpkin mixture. Pile into pie shell. Top with Honey Graham Cracker crumbs. Chill until firm.

Yield: One 9-in. (23-cm) pie

Kiwi Cream Pie

2 recipes	French Vanilla Pudding (p. 126)	2 recipes
2 c.	Crisp Topping (p. 105)	500 mL
2 T.	sweet butter (melted)	30 mL
4	kiwis (peeled and sliced)	4

Prepare French Vanilla Pudding. Combine 1½ c. (375 mL) of the Crisp Topping and melted butter in bowl. Stir to mix. Press into bottom and sides of 10-in. (25-cm) pie pan. Bake at 300° F (150° C) for 15 minutes. Cool completely. Arrange ⅓ of kiwi slices over topping in pie pan. Spoon in ½ of pudding mixture. Sprinkle with ¼ c. (60 mL) of topping. Repeat with ⅓ of kiwi slices, and the remaining pudding, and remaining topping. Decorate with remaining kiwi slices. Chill thoroughly.

Yield: One 10-in. (25-cm) pie

Rhubarb Kuchen

Crust:

1 c.	all-purpose flour	250 mL
½ c.	sweet butter	125 mL
¼ t.	salt	1 mL
2 T.	sugar	30 mL
1	egg yolk	1

Mix ingredients thoroughly. Pat into 9-in. (23-cm) square pan.

Filling:

1 qt.	rhubarb (sliced)	1 L
2	eggs	2
1 c.	sugar	250 mL
1 T.	all-purpose flour	15 mL

Combine ingredients; mix thoroughly. Pour into crust. Bake at 350° F (175° C) for 35 to 40 minutes or until set.

Microwave: Cook on Medium for 12 to 15 minutes. Turn dish a quarter turn every 5 minutes. Allow to rest 5 minutes or until set.

Yield: 9 servings

Mango Nut Dessert

2 c.	Crisp Topping (p. 105)	500 mL
3	mangoes (peeled and sliced)	3
½ c.	nutmeats (not almonds)	125 mL
2 T.	sugar	30 mL
½ t.	nutmeg	2 mL

Pat 1½ c. (375 mL) of the Crisp Topping evenly in bottom of 8-in. (20-cm) square pan. Place mango slices on top; sprinkle with nuts, sugar, and nutmeg. Top with remaining ½ c. (125 mL) topping. Bake at 350° F (175° C) for 30 minutes. Serve with whipped cream.

Yield: 5 to 6 servings

Rhubarb Treat

3 c.	rhubarb (sliced)	750 mL
1½ c.	sugar	375 mL
½ t.	pure vanilla extract	2 mL
1 c.	all-purpose flour	250 mL
1 c.	brown sugar (packed)	250 mL
½ c.	pure solid shortening	125 mL
½ c.	milk	125 mL
1	egg	1
½ t.	baking powder	2 mL
¼ t.	salt	1 mL

Combine rhubarb, 1½ c. (375 mL) sugar, and the vanilla extract in mixing bowl. Toss to coat. Allow to rest 5 minutes. Pour into greased 9-in. (23-cm) square pan. Combine remaining ingredients. Stir to blend thoroughly. Spread over rhubarb. Bake at 375° F (190° C) for 40 to 45 minutes. Serve hot or cold.

Yield: 8 to 10 servings

Pineapple Cheesecake

9-in.	Graham Cracker Pie Shell mixture (p. 108)	23-cm
½ c.	water (cold)	125 mL
2 env.	unflavored gelatin	2 env.
3	eggs (separated)	3
1 c.	sugar	250 mL
½ c.	water (cold)	125 mL
3 T.	lemon juice	45 mL
2 pkg. (8 oz. each)	cream cheese (softened)	2 pkg. (226 g each)
1 c.	whipped heavy cream	250 mL
1 lb.	crushed pineapple (drained)	500 g

Press Graham Cracker Pie Shell mixture into well-greased 9-in. (23-cm) springform pan. Chill. Combine ½ c. (125 mL) cold water with gelatin. Allow to soften 5 minutes. Beat egg yolks in medium saucepan. Add sugar and ½ c. (125 mL) cold water. Cook and stir over medium heat until slightly thickened. Add lemon juice and gelatin mixture; stir until completely dissolved and blended. Beat cream cheese until fluffy; gradually add egg yolk mixture, beating constantly until smooth. Chill until firm. Whip egg whites until stiff. Gently fold in whipped cream, whipped egg whites and drained pineapple into cheese mixture. Pour into chilled prepared pan. Chill until firmly set. Remove sides of pan. If desired, garnish with pecan or walnut pieces.

Yield: One 9-in. (23-cm) cake

Kiwi Cottage Torte

2 c.	Crisp Topping (p. 105)	500 mL
4 c.	cottage cheese	1 L
3	egg yolks	3
1	egg	1
½ c.	sugar	125 mL
½ c.	hazelnuts (ground)	125 mL
2 T.	lemon juice	30 mL
1 T.	all-purpose flour	15 mL
2 t.	pure vanilla extract	10 mL
2 t.	lemon peel (grated)	10 mL
dash	salt	dash
4	kiwis (peeled and sliced)	4
¼ c.	honey	60 mL
1 t.	water	5 mL
½ t.	lemon juice	2 mL

Press Crisp Topping into bottom and 2 in. (5 cm) up sides of 9-in. (23-cm) springform pan. Combine cottage cheese, egg yolks, egg, sugar, nuts, 2 T. (30 mL) lemon juice, flour, vanilla extract, lemon peel, and salt in bowl, blender, or food processor. Blend or whip until smooth. Pour over topping in pan. Bake at 350° F (175° C) for 60 to 65 minutes, or until set and top is golden. Arrange kiwi slices decoratively on top. Combine honey, water, and ½ t. (2 mL) lemon juice in small bowl. Brush kiwi slices lightly with honey mixture.

Yield: 10 to 12 servings

Rhubarb Crisp

6 c.	rhubarb (sliced)	1500 mL
1½ c.	sugar	375 mL
1 t.	cinnamon	5 mL
1 t.	pure vanilla extract	5 mL
3 c.	Crisp Topping (p. 105)	750 mL

Spread rhubarb evenly in bottom of 13 × 9-in. (33 × 23-cm) pan. Sprinkle with sugar, cinnamon, and vanilla extract. Cover with Crisp Topping. Bake at 350° F (175° C) for 30 minutes.

Yield: 10 to 12 servings

Thumbprint Pastry

1 pkg.	yeast	1 pkg.
¼ c.	water (lukewarm)	60 mL
1 c.	milk (scalded)	250 mL
¼ c.	sugar	60 mL
⅓ c.	shortening	90 mL
1 t.	salt	5 mL
1	egg	1
3 to 4 c.	all-purpose flour	750 to 1000 mL

Dissolve yeast in lukewarm water; set aside. Beat scalded milk, sugar, shortening, and salt. Add egg and 2 c. (500 mL) of the flour. Beat to blend. Stir in remaining flour to make a soft dough. Cover; set in warm place to rise until double in size. Dust hands with flour. Pinch off enough dough to make a small biscuit. Make an indentation in the center of each with the thumb. Fill with filling of your choice (pp. 147–148). Allow to rest 10 to 15 minutes. Bake at 350° F (175° C) for 15 to 20 minutes or until golden brown. Brush with melted sweet butter. If desired, sprinkle with topping of your choice (p. 148).

Yield: 2 to 3 dozen thumbprint pastries

Fillings for Thumbprint Pastry

Prepare one of the following and spoon into indentation:

COTTAGE CHEESE

½ c.	cottage cheese	125 mL
1	egg yolk	1
1 T.	sugar	15 mL

Mix thoroughly.

LEMON COTTAGE CHEESE

½ c.	cottage cheese	125 mL
1	egg yolk	1
1 T.	sugar	15 mL
1 t.	lemon peel	5 mL
½ t.	lemon juice	2 mL

Mix thoroughly.

PINEAPPLE COTTAGE CHEESE

½ c.	cottage cheese	125 mL
1	egg yolk	1
1 t.	sugar	5 mL
¼ c.	crushed pineapple	60 mL

Mix thoroughly.

PINEAPPLE

½ c.	crushed pineapple	125 mL
1 t.	sugar	5 mL
1 t.	cornstarch	5 mL
dash	salt	dash

Cook over low heat 5 minutes; allow to cool slightly.

POPPY SEED

½ c.	poppy seeds	125 mL
¼ c.	sugar	60 mL
¼ c.	milk	60 mL
½ t.	pure vanilla extract	2 mL

Cook over low heat 5 minutes; allow to cool slightly.

(fillings for Thumbprint Pastry, cont.)

CARROT

½ c.	carrot (grated)	125 mL
2 t.	sugar	10 mL
1 t.	cinnamon	5 mL
1 t.	cornstarch	5 mL
2 T.	water	30 mL

Cook over low heat 5 minutes; allow to cool slightly.

WALNUT or PECAN

½ c.	nuts (ground)	125 mL
¼ c.	water	60 mL
2 t.	sugar	10 mL
1 t.	pure vanilla extract	5 mL
1 t.	cornstarch	5 mL

Cook over low heat 5 minutes; allow to cool slightly.

Toppings for Thumbprint Pastry

Allow pastries to completely cool. Dust tops with sifted powdered sugar, or prepare one of the following:

CRUMB

¼ c.	all-purpose flour	125 mL
¼ c.	sugar	125 mL
½ t.	sweet butter	2 mL
½ t.	pure vanilla extract	2 mL

Work into crumbs. Sprinkle over tops.

SUGAR GLAZE

¼ c.	sugar	60 mL
2 T.	water (hot)	30 mL

Dissolve sugar in hot water. Gently brush tops of thumbprint pastry. Allow to dry.

FROZEN DESSERTS AND CANDIES

Lemon, Lime, or Grapefruit Sugar Cubes

	peel from 1 fruit	
10 to 12	sugar cubes	10 to 12

Place ½ of peel into jar; add sugar cubes. Cover with remaining peel. Cover jar tightly. Allow to stand at room temperature (if not too hot) for 5 to 6 days. The sugar cubes become fruit-flavored candy. The peel may then be discarded, or more sugar cubes may be added to start a second batch.

Mango Ice

1 env.	unflavored gelatin	1 env.
¾ c.	sugar	190 mL
2 c.	water	500 mL
2 c.	mango (juice and pulp)	500 mL
1 T.	lemon juice	15 mL
2	egg whites (beaten)	2

Combine gelatin, sugar, and water in saucepan; cook and stir over low heat until gelatin and sugar are completely dissolved. Add mango juice and pulp, and lemon juice; stir to blend. Pour into freezer trays or metal cake pans; freeze until mushy. Pour mixture into large mixing bowl; beat until fluffy. Fold in beaten egg whites. Return to freezer trays or freezer boxes. Freeze firm.

Yield: 1½ qt. (1.5 L)

Mango Cake Roll

4	eggs (separated)	4
1 c.	sugar	250 mL
1 t.	pure vanilla extract	5 mL
¾ c.	all-purpose flour (sifted)	190 mL
¾ t.	baking powder	4 mL
¼ t.	salt	1 mL
½ recipe	Mango Ice Cream (p. 155)	½ recipe

Beat egg yolks until light and lemon colored. Gradually beat in sugar. Beat until stiff. Add vanilla extract; mix thoroughly. Continue beating; gradually add flour, baking powder and salt. Beat egg whites until stiff. Fold into cake batter. Spread onto 15 × 10-in. (39 × 25-cm) jelly-roll pan, which has been lined with parchment or waxed paper. Bake at 375° F (190° C) for 15 minutes or until toothpick inserted in center comes out clean. Turn out onto towel sprinkled with confectioners' sugar. Remove paper; cut away dry edges of cake. Roll up cake and towel, jelly-roll style. Cool completely. Carefully unroll and remove towel; spread cake with softened Mango Ice Cream. Reroll; wrap in plastic wrap. Freeze until firm.

Yield: 12 to 14 servings

Pineapple Sherbet

1 env.	unflavored gelatin	1 env.
1½ c.	pure pineapple juice	375 mL
½ c.	sugar	125 mL
2	eggs (separated)	2
2 c.	milk	500 mL

Soften gelatin in pineapple juice 5 minutes. Add sugar; cook over medium heat until gelatin and sugar are dissolved. Add egg yolks and milk; stir to blend. Pour into freezer trays; freeze until firm. Remove from trays; break into chunks and beat until smooth. Beat egg whites until stiff. Fold into pineapple mixture. Return to freezer trays. Freeze firm.

Yield: 8 to 12 servings

Banana Honey Sherbet

1 env.	unflavored gelatin	1 env.
¼ c.	honey	60 mL
2 c.	milk	500 mL
3	bananas (mashed)	3
2	egg whites (stiffly beaten)	2

Combine gelatin, honey, and milk in saucepan. Cook over low heat until gelatin is dissolved and honey blended. Add bananas. Pour into freezer trays or metal cake pans. Freeze until mushy. Beat until fluffy or double in size. Fold in beaten egg whites. Return to freezer trays or freezer boxes. Freeze firm.

Yield: 1½ qt. (1.5 L)

Lemon or Lime Sherbet

1 env.	unflavored gelatin	1 env.
1½ c.	sugar	375 mL
2 c.	water	500 mL
2 c.	milk	500 mL
¾ c.	lemon or lime juice	190 mL
2 t.	lemon or lime peel (grated)	10 mL
	optional: pure or homemade food coloring (p. 20)	
2	egg whites (stiffly beaten)	2

Combine gelatin, sugar, and water in saucepan; heat and stir over low heat until gelatin and sugar are completely dissolved. Remove from heat. Add milk, juice, and peel. Add food coloring, if desired. Stir to blend. Pour into freezer trays or metal cake pans. Freeze until mushy. Pour mixture into large mixing bowl. Beat until fluffy; fold in beaten egg whites. Return to freezer trays or freezer boxes; freeze firm.

Yield: 1½ qt. (1.5 L)

Easy Papaya Ice

1½ c.	papaya (puréed)	375 mL
2 c.	milk	500 mL
¾ c.	honey	190 mL
3 T.	lemon juice	45 mL
1 T.	lemon peel	15 mL

Combine all ingredients in blender or food processor. Blend until smooth. Pour into freezer trays or metal cake pan. Freeze firm. To serve, cut with warm, sharp knife.

Yield: 1 qt. (1 L)

Watermelon Popsicles

1 t.	unflavored gelatin	5 mL
2 T.	sugar	10 mL
1 c.	water (boiling)	250 mL
1½ c.	watermelon juice (p. 159)	375 mL

Combine gelatin and sugar in bowl or pitcher. Add boiling water; stir to completely dissolve. Cool slightly. Blend in Watermelon Juice. Pour into popsicle forms or 5-oz. (150-g) paper cups. Freeze.

Yield: 8 popsicles

Banana Popsicles

1 t.	unflavored gelatin	5 mL
2 T.	sugar	30 mL
2½ c.	water	625 mL
2	bananas (mashed)	2

Sprinkle gelatin and sugar into water in saucepan. Allow to soften 2 to 3 minutes. Stir to dissolve. Bring to boil. Remove from heat; add mashed bananas. Allow to cool slightly. Pour into blender or food processor. Blend until liquid. Pour into popsicle molds or 5-oz. (150-g) paper cups. Freeze.

Yield: 8 popsicles

Cantaloupe Popsicles

1½ c.	water	375 mL
2 t.	sugar	10 mL
1 t.	unflavored gelatin	5 mL
1 c.	cantaloupe pulp	250 mL
dash	salt	dash

Combine water and sugar in saucepan. Sprinkle gelatin on top. Allow to soften 2 to 3 minutes. Stir to dissolve sugar and gelatin. Bring to boil. Remove from heat. Add cantaloupe pulp and salt. Allow to cool and partially set. Stir to blend. Pour into popsicle molds or 5-oz. (150-g) paper cups. Freeze.

Yield: 8 popsicles

Grapefruit or Lemon Popsicles

2 c.	water	500 mL
½ c.	lemon juice	125 mL
¼ c.	sugar	60 mL
dash	salt	dash
1 t.	unflavored gelatin	5 mL
	optional: pure or homemade yellow food coloring (p. 20)	

Combine water, lemon juice, sugar, and salt in saucepan. Sprinkle gelatin over top. Allow to soften 2 to 3 minutes. Stir to dissolve gelatin, sugar, and salt. Bring to boil. Remove from heat. Add food coloring, if desired. Cool. Pour into popsicle molds or 5-oz. (150-g) paper cups. Freeze.

Yield: 8 popsicles

Lime Popsicles

2 c.	water	500 mL	
½ c.	lime juice	125 mL	
¾ c.	sugar	190 mL	
1 t.	unflavored gelatin	5 mL	
	optional: pure or homemade green food coloring (p. 20)		

Combine water, lime juice, and sugar in saucepan. Sprinkle gelatin over top. Allow to soften 2 to 3 minutes. Stir to dissolve sugar and gelatin. Bring to boil. Remove from heat. Add food coloring, if desired. Cool. Pour into popsicle molds or 5-oz. (150-g) paper cups. Freeze.

Yield: 8 popsicles

Lemon Torte

24	pure or homemade Honey Graham Crackers (p. 107)	24	
¼ c.	sweet butter (melted)	60 mL	
2	eggs	2	
¼ c.	honey	60 mL	
¾ c.	corn syrup	190 mL	
2 c.	buttermilk	500 mL	
½ c.	lemon juice	125 mL	
1 T.	lemon peel (grated)	15 mL	

Crush Honey Graham Crackers. Add melted butter and blend. Press into bottom and sides of 9-in. (23-cm) springform pan. Chill thoroughly. Beat eggs until frothy; continue beating, gradually adding honey and corn syrup. Beat until mixture is thick. Fold in buttermilk, lemon juice, and lemon peel. Pour into freezer tray or metal cake pan. Freeze until mushy. Beat until fluffy. Pour into graham cracker crust. Freeze firm.

Yield: 10 to 12 servings

Mango Ice Cream

1 c.	sugar	250 mL
2 t.	cornstarch	10 mL
1 qt.	milk (cold)	1 L
3	eggs (separated)	3
1 t.	pure vanilla extract	5 mL
1½ c.	mango (puréed)	325 mL
1 c.	whipped heavy cream	250 mL

Combine sugar, cornstarch, cold milk, and egg yolks in saucepan. Beat until frothy. Stir and cook over low heat until thickened. Remove from heat; stir in vanilla extract and mango purée. Cool. Beat egg whites until stiff. Fold in egg whites. Pour into freezer trays or metal cake pans. Freeze until mushy. Beat until fluffy. Fold in whipped cream. Return to freezer trays or freezer boxes. Freeze firm.

Yield: 1½ to 2 qt. (1.5 to 2 L)

Vanilla Ice Cream

1 c.	sugar	250 mL
2 t.	cornstarch	10 mL
1 qt.	milk (cold)	1 L
4	egg yolks	4
1 T.	pure vanilla extract	15 mL
2 c.	whipped heavy cream	500 mL

Combine sugar, cornstarch, cold milk, and egg yolks in saucepan. Whip to blend. Stir and cook over low heat until thickened. Remove from heat; add vanilla extract. Cool. Fold into whipped cream. Pour into freezer trays. Freeze until mushy. Beat until fluffy. Return to freezer trays. Freeze firm. (An ice-cream freezer may be used, if desired.)

Yield: 1½ qt. (1.5 L)

Vanilla Honey Ice Cream

1 c.	honey	250 mL
2 t.	cornstarch	10 mL
1 qt.	milk (cold)	1 L
3	eggs (separated)	3
2 t.	pure vanilla extract	10 mL
1 c.	whipped heavy cream	250 mL

Combine honey, cornstarch, cold milk, and egg yolks in saucepan. Whip to blend. Stir and cook over low heat until thickened. Remove from heat. Stir in vanilla extract. Cool. Beat egg whites into soft peaks; fold into honey mixture. Pour into freezer trays or metal cake pans. Freeze until mushy. Beat until fluffy. Beat in whipped cream. Pour into freezer trays or freezer boxes. Freeze firm.

Yield: 1½ qt. (1.5 L)

Cotton Candy Bites

3	egg whites	3
¼ t.	cream of tartar	2 mL
1 c.	sugar	250 mL
1 t.	lemon peel (grated)	5 mL

Beat egg whites and cream of tartar until stiff. Gradually add sugar and lemon peel. Beat until sugar is well blended. Drop by small spoonfuls onto very lightly greased cookie sheets. Bake at 325° F (165° C) for 15 to 20 minutes.

Yield: 70 to 80 bites

Cream Caramels

2 c.	sugar	500 mL
¾ c.	white corn syrup	190 mL
½ c.	sweet butter	125 mL
2 c.	light cream	500 mL

Combine sugar, syrup, butter, and 1 c. (250 mL) of the cream in saucepan. Bring to a boil. Remove from heat. Add remaining cream; stir well. Return to heat. Cook over medium heat to hard ball stage (260° F; 125° C). Pour into well-greased baking sheet. Cool slightly. Score into squares or roll into balls.

Yield: 4 to 5 dozen caramels

Candy Bars

1 c.	sugar	250 mL
¾ c.	all-purpose flour	190 mL.
1 t.	baking powder	5 mL
½ t.	salt	2 mL
1 c.	dates (floured and chopped)	250 mL
1 c.	peanuts (chopped)	250 mL
2	eggs (slightly beaten)	2

Mix and sift dry ingredients twice. Blend in dates and nuts. Add eggs. Mix thoroughly. Spread into well-greased 8-in. (20-cm) pan. Bake at 350° F (175° C) for 25 to 30 minutes. Cool thoroughly. Cut into bars.

Yield: 8 2″ x 4″ (5 cm x 10 cm) bars

Pineapple Fudge

2 c.	sugar	500 mL
½ c.	crushed pineapple (drained)	125 mL
½ c.	light cream	125 mL
1 T.	sweet butter	15 mL
1 c.	pecans or walnuts	250 mL

Combine sugar, pineapple, cream, and butter in saucepan. Cook to soft ball stage (240° F; 115° C). Add nuts; beat until thick. Pour into well-greased 9-in. (23-cm) square pan. Cut into 1-in. (2.5-cm) pieces when cool.

Yield: 81 pieces

Marshmallow Creme

2	egg whites	2
½ c.	sugar	125 mL
1 c.	light corn syrup	250 mL
¼ c.	water	60 mL
⅛ t.	cream of tartar	.5 mL
¼ t.	salt	1 mL
1 t.	pure vanilla extract	5 mL

Whip egg whites until very stiff; set aside. Combine sugar, syrup, water, cream of tartar, and salt in saucepan. Cook until thread stage (230° F; 100° C). Pour slowly into egg whites. Beat until stiff; add vanilla extract.

Yield: 2 c. (500 mL)

JAMS, JELLIES, AND PRESERVES

Honeydew Jam

1	honeydew melon	1
3 c.	water	375 mL
2 T.	lemon juice	30 mL
2 t.	lemon rind	10 mL
2 c.	sugar	500 mL

Peel, seed, and chop melon. Place pulp into non-aluminum pan. Add water, lemon juice, and lemon rind. Heat to boiling; cook until melon is transparent. Add sugar; cook to desired thickness. Pour into sterilized jars; seal.

Microwave: Same as above. Cook on Medium-Low.

Yield: 3 c. (750 mL)

Watermelon

2 to 3 c.	watermelon cubes	500 to 750 mL

Place watermelon cubes in blender or food processor. Blend thoroughly. Pour through strainer. Reserve juice. Remove any seeds from strainer. Reserve pulp.

Juice Yield: 1¼ to 1½ c. (310 to 375 mL)
Pulp Yield: ½ to ¾ c. (125 to 190 mL)

Hawaiian Chutney

4 lb.	pineapple (cleaned and cubed)	2 kg
2 c.	pears (peeled and cubed)	500 mL
2 c.	coconut (cubed)	500 mL
1 c.	dates (chopped)	250 mL
1 c.	distilled white vinegar	250 mL
½ c.	coconut milk	125 mL
1 c.	brown sugar (packed)	250 mL
1 clove	garlic (minced)	1 clove
1 t.	cinnamon	5 mL
½ t.	nutmeg	2 mL
½ c.	pecans	125 mL

Combine all ingredients (except pecans) in saucepan. Bring to boil. Reduce heat; cook and stir over medium heat until desired thickness. Remove from heat. Stir in pecans. Ladle into hot sterilized jars. Seal tightly.

Yield: 2 qt. (2 L)

Pineapple Chutney

2 lb.	pineapple	1 kg
½ c.	distilled white vinegar	125 mL
2 T.	dry mustard	30 mL
1	onion (chopped)	1
1	celery stalk (chopped)	1
1½ c.	sugar	375 mL
¼ t.	ginger	1 mL
¼ t.	garlic powder	1 mL

Peel, core, and dice pineapple. Place in large pot with vinegar and dry mustard. Cook over low heat until pineapple is softened. Press through food mill or blend in food processor or blender. Pour pineapple back into pot; add remaining ingredients. Boil over low heat, stirring constantly, for 10 minutes. Remove from heat. Allow to cool completely. Return to heat; bring to boil. Cook and stir 5 minutes more or until very thick. Pour into sterilized jars and seal.

Yield: Five 6-oz. (170-mL) jars

Watermelon Pickles

2 lb.	watermelon rind	1 kg
¼ c.	salt	60 mL
1 qt.	water	1 L
4 c.	sugar	1 L
2 c.	distilled white vinegar	500 mL
2 c.	water	500 mL
1	lemon (sliced)	1
2	cinnamon sticks (broken)	2

Peel, clean, and cut rind into 1 to 1½-in. (3 to 4-cm) pieces. Combine salt and 1 qt. (1 L) water; add rind. Allow to soak overnight. (More water may be added if necessary to cover rind.) Drain and rinse. Place in large kettle or saucepan. Cover with water; cook over medium heat until rind is translucent. Drain. Combine sugar, vinegar, 2 c. (500 mL) water, lemon, and cinnamon sticks in kettle. Bring to boil; reduce heat and simmer 10 to 15 minutes. Strain liquid. Add rind to liquid; simmer until liquid is clear. Fill sterilized jars. Seal.

Yield: 3 pt. (1½ L)

Sweet Relish

1 qt.	watermelon rind (cubed)	1 L
1 qt.	onion (cubed)	1 L
1 qt.	cabbage (cut in pieces)	1 L
2 c.	celery (chopped)	500 mL
6 c.	sugar	1500 mL
2 c.	distilled white vinegar	500 mL
2 c.	water	500 mL
½ c.	salt	125 mL
2 t.	mustard seeds	10 mL
1½ t.	turmeric	7 mL

Combine rind, onion, cabbage, and celery. Chop coarsely in food processor or use food grinder. Place in large bowl. Cover with remaining ingredients. Stir to blend. Allow to rest overnight. Bring to boil; reduce heat. Simmer for 20 minutes. Pack relish mixture into sterilized jars. Seal tightly.

Yield: 2 qt. (2 L)

Vegetable Relish

1 head	cabbage	1 head
10	onions	10
1 large	zucchini	1 large
5	turnips	5
10	carrots	10
½ c.	salt	125 mL
6 c.	sugar	1500 mL
2 T.	mustard seeds	30 mL
1 T.	celery seeds	15 mL
1½ t.	turmeric	7 mL
3 c.	distilled white vinegar	750 mL
3 c.	water	750 mL

Clean and chop all vegetables. Place in large glass bowl. Sprinkle with salt; stir to mix. Cover with water; allow to stand overnight. Drain and rinse thoroughly. Place vegetables in large pan. Add sugar, mustard seeds, celery seeds, turmeric, vinegar, and 3 c. (750 mL) water. Heat to boiling; reduce heat and simmer 3 minutes. Fill sterilized jars. Seal.

Yield: 5 to 6 pt. (3 L)

Corn Relish

5 c.	corn	1250 mL
4	onions (chopped fine)	4
1 head	cabbage (chopped fine)	1 head
2 c.	distilled white vinegar	500 mL
2½ c.	sugar	625 mL
¼ c.	salt	60 mL
2 t.	pepper	10 mL

Combine all ingredients in saucepan. Bring to boil. Boil 20 minutes. Pack in sterilized jars. Seal tightly.

Yield: 2 qt. (2 L)

Bread and Butter Slices

4 qt.	watermelon rind (peel and pink removed)	4 L
6	onions (sliced)	6
3 cloves	garlic	3 cloves
⅓ c.	salt	90 mL
5 c.	sugar	1250 mL
2 c.	distilled white vinegar	500 mL
1 c.	lemon juice	250 mL
2 T.	mustard seeds	30 mL
1½ t.	turmeric	7 mL
1½ t.	celery seeds	7 mL

Slice watermelon rind thin. Place in large bowl or container. Add onions and whole garlic cloves. Add salt. Stir to mix. Cover with cracked ice. Refrigerate for 3 hours. Drain well. Combine remaining ingredients. Pour over rind. Heat just to boiling. Pack in hot sterilized jars. Seal tightly.

Yield: 4 qt. (4 L)

Watermelon Sticks

6 lb.	watermelon rind (peel and pink removed)	3 kg
36 small	onions	36 small
6 stalks	celery	6 stalks
2 T.	mustard seeds	30 mL
3 qt.	distilled white vinegar	3 L
3 c.	sugar	750 mL
1 c.	salt	250 mL

Cut rind into 5-in. (12-cm) stalks. Cover watermelon rind with ice water. Allow to soak for 3 to 4 hours. Drain. Pack into six sterilized 1-qt. (1-L) jars. Add 6 onions, 1 stalk celery, and 1 t. (5 mL) mustard seeds to each jar. Combine vinegar, sugar, and salt in saucepan. Bring to boil. Pour over watermelon rinds. Seal jars tightly.

Yield: 6 qt. (6 L)

Sweet Dill Sticks

	watermelon rind	
	(cut to desired width and length)	
3 or 4 slices	onion	3 or 4 slices
3 or 4 heads	dill	3 or 4 heads
2 c.	water	500 mL
2 c.	distilled white vinegar	500 mL
1 c.	sugar	500 mL
¼ c.	salt	60 mL

Sterilize three or four 1-qt. (1-L) jars. Pack watermelon sticks in each jar. Add onion slice and head of dill to each jar. Combine water, vinegar, sugar, and salt in saucepan. Bring to a boil. Divide among jars. Seal tightly.

Yield: 3 to 4 qt. (3 to 4 L)

Kosher Dill Sticks

4 lb.	watermelon rind (peel and pink removed)	2 kg
6 cloves	garlic	6 cloves
6	bay leaves	6
¾ c.	dill seeds	190 mL
¼ c.	mustard seeds	60 mL
3 c.	distilled white vinegar	750 mL
3 c.	water	750 mL
⅓ c.	salt	90 mL

Cut rind into 4-in. (10-cm) sticks. Pack into six 2-c. (500-mL) sterilized jars. Add 1 clove garlic, 1 bay leaf, 2 T. (30 mL) dill seeds, and 2 t. (10 mL) mustard seeds to each jar. Combine vinegar, water, and salt. Bring to boil. Divide among jars. Seal jars tightly.

Yield: Six 2-c. (500-mL) jars

Pickled Mangoes

3 lb.	sugar	1.5 kg
2 c.	distilled white vinegar	500 mL
1 c.	lemon juice	250 mL
1 c.	water	250 mL
6 lb.	fresh mangoes	3 kg

Boil sugar, vinegar, lemon juice, and water until sugar is dissolved. Peel mangoes. Add to the syrup and cook until fork-tender. Pack in sterilized jars and fill with pickling liquid. Seal jars tightly.

Yield: 3 qt. (3 L)

BEVERAGES

Chocolate Eggnog

4	eggs (separated)	4
½ c.	sugar	125 mL
3 c.	milk	750 mL
¼ c.	Chocolate Syrup (p. 94)	60 mL
1 t.	pure vanilla extract	5 mL
dash	salt	dash

Beat egg yolks and ¼ c. (60 mL) of the sugar until thick and creamy; gradually add milk, Chocolate Syrup, vanilla extract, and salt. Beat until frothy. Beat egg whites and remaining sugar until stiff. Fold into egg-yolk mixture. Serve in mugs.

Yield: 6 to 7 servings

Lemonade

4	lemons	4
2½ c.	sugar	625 mL
4 qt.	water	4 L

Cut lemons (unpeeled) into pieces. Place in blender or food processor. Add ½ c. (125 mL) water. Blend until smooth. Strain into large pitcher or pan, pushing on pulp to extract all the juice. Stir in sugar and remaining water.

Yield: 4 qt. (4 L)

Cranberry Juice

1 qt.	water	1 L
1 c.	sugar	250 mL
2 c.	cranberries	500 mL

Combine water and sugar in saucepan; stir and cook over medium heat until sugar is dissolved. Add cranberries; cook until all skins are popped. Simmer 5 minutes longer. Remove from heat; strain and chill.

Yield: 1 qt. (1 L)

Cranberry Juice Cocktail

½ c.	pure or homemade Cranberry Juice (p. 167)	125 mL
¼ c.	pineapple juice	60 mL
1 t.	lemon juice	5 mL
1 c.	ice (crushed)	250 mL
	pineapple chunks	

Combine juices and ice in blender or food processor. Blend until slush. Serve in cocktail glasses. Garnish each glass with pineapple chunks.

Yield: 2 c. (500 mL)

Mango Freeze

1 c.	mango (diced)	250 mL
½ c.	milk (cold)	125 mL
1 t.	confectioners' sugar	5 mL
½ t.	pure vanilla extract	2 mL
6 to 8	ice cubes	6 to 8

Combine mango, cold milk, sugar, and vanilla extract in blender or food processor. Blend until smooth. Add ice cubes, one at a time, until thick and frosty.

Yield: 1 serving

Spiced Milk

1 c.	milk	250 mL
1 t.	sugar	5 mL
dash	cinnamon and nutmeg	dash
	whipped cream	

Combine milk, sugar, and spices in saucepan; heat to steaming. Pour into large mug. Top with whipped cream.

Yield: 1 serving

Party Punch

10	lemons (cut up)	10
5	limes (cut up)	5
1 qt.	water	1 L
2½ c.	sugar	625 mL
1 qt.	grapefruit juice	1 L
1 qt.	pineapple juice	1 L
2 qt.	7-Up®	2 L
	ice ring, lemon slices, lime slices	

Combine lemons, limes, and 2 c. (500 mL) of the water in blender or food processor. Blend to pulp stage. Pour into saucepan; add remaining water and the sugar. Stir and heat to boiling. Strain; discard pulp. Cool. Just before serving, combine lemon-lime juice, grapefruit juice, pineapple juice, and 7-Up®; stir to blend. Pour into punch bowl. Add ice ring and fruit slices.

Yield: 6 qt. (6 L)

Lime Float

1 c.	pure limeade	250 mL
¾ c.	pure or homemade Lime Sherbet (p. 151)	190 mL

Pour limeade into tall glass. Add ¼ c. (60 mL) of Lime Sherbet. Stir to blend. Top with remaining sherbet.

Yield: 1 serving

Banana Pineapple Cooler

1	banana (ripe)	1
1 c.	pineapple juice (cold)	250 mL
½ c.	milk (cold)	125 mL
3 to 4	ice cubes	3 to 4

Combine banana, cold pineapple juice, and cold milk in blender or food processor. Blend until smooth. Add ice cubes one at a time. Blend until ice is crushed.

Yield: 2 c. (500 mL)

Grapefruit Punch

1 qt.	grapefruit juice	1 L
2 c.	7-Up®	500 mL
2 c.	pure or homemade Lemon Sherbet (p. 151)	500 mL
	lemon slices	

Combine grapefruit juice and 7-Up® in punch bowl. Top with Lemon Sherbet and lemon slices.

Yield: 1¾ qt. (1.7 L)

Piña Punch

1 qt.	pineapple juice	1 L
1 c.	unsweetened coconut (grated)	250 mL
¼ c.	confectioners' sugar	60 mL
2 c.	7-Up®	500 mL
	ice ring	

Combine 1 c. (250 mL) of the pineapple juice, the coconut, and sugar in blender or food processor. Blend thoroughly. Pour into punch bowl; add remaining pineapple juice. Just before serving, add 7-Up® and ice ring.

Yield: 1½ qt. (1.5 L)

Mango Cooler

½ c.	mango (juice and pulp)	125 mL
1 c.	milk (cold)	250 mL
½ c.	whipped heavy cream	125 mL

Combine mango juice and cold milk. Stir into whipped cream. Pour into glasses; top with extra whipped cream.

Yield: 1¾ c. (440 mL)

French Chocolate Drink

1 c.	milk (cold)	250 mL
½ c.	pure or homemade Chocolate Syrup (p. 94)	125 mL
2	egg yolks	2
1 c.	whipped heavy cream	250 mL
	additional whipped cream	

Combine cold milk, Chocolate Syrup, and egg yolks in blender or food processor. Whip until smooth. Fold into whipped cream. Serve in wide-mouth glasses. Top with additional whipped cream.

Yield: 2½ c. (625 mL)

Peanut Surprise

2 c.	milk (cold)	500 mL
1 c.	skinless peanuts	250 mL
½ c.	sugar	125 mL
¼ c.	honey	60 mL
1 t.	pure vanilla extract	5 mL
dash	salt	dash

Combine all ingredients in blender or food processor. Whip until well blended. Serve.

Yield: 3 c. (750 mL)

Coconut Dandy

1 c.	milk (cold)	250 mL
½ c.	unsweetened coconut (grated)	125 mL
1 T.	confectioners' sugar	15 mL
½ t.	pure vanilla extract	2 mL

Combine ingredients in blender. Blend thoroughly. Pour into tall glass.

Yield: 1 serving

Grapefruit Freeze

1 c.	grapefruit (juice and pulp)	250 mL
¼ c.	honey	60 mL
6	ice cubes	6

Combine grapefruit and honey in blender or food processor. Blend thoroughly; add ice cubes, one at a time. Blend until slush.

Yield: 1 serving

Lemon Frost

½ c.	pure or homemade Lemonade (p. 166)	125 mL
½ c.	milk (cold)	125 mL
1 c.	pure or homemade Lemon Sherbet (p. 151)	250 mL
	whipped cream	

Combine Lemonade, cold milk, and Lemon Sherbet in bowl or blender. Whip until smooth. Pour into glasses. Top with whipped cream.

Yield: 2 c. (500 mL)

Avocado Crystals

1	avocado (diced)	1
2 c.	grapefruit juice	500 mL
½ c.	sugar	125 mL
½ t.	nutmeg	2 mL
¼ t.	salt	1 mL

Combine ingredients in blender or food processor. Blend until smooth. Pour into freezer trays. Freeze until firm. Return to blender or food processor. Whip just until mixed. Serve.

Yield: 3 c. (750 mL)

Pineapple-Coconut Cooler

2 qt.	crushed ice	2 L
1 qt.	fresh pineapple (cubed)	1 L
2 c.	pineapple juice	500 mL
2 c.	fresh coconut (shredded)	500 mL
1 c.	milk	250 mL

Combine ingredients in large bowl. In batches, pour into blender and mix thoroughly. Pour into large glass refrigerator containers. Serve cold.

Yield: 3½ qt. (3½ L)

Mulled Cranberry Drink

¾ c.	cranberry juice	190 mL
1 slice	lemon	1 slice
1 t.	nutmeg	5 mL
1 T.	honey	15 mL
	cinnamon stick	

Heat cranberry juice, lemon slice, nutmeg, and honey. DO NOT BOIL. Serve with cinnamon stick.

Yield: 1 c. (250 mL)

HOLIDAY FARE

STUFFED PUMPKIN

1 small	pumpkin	1 small
¼ c.	water	60 mL
3 T.	sweet butter	45 mL
1 T.	honey	15 mL
¼ t.	salt	1 mL
½ t.	cinnamon	2 mL
¼ t.	nutmeg	1 mL
	pineapple chunks	

To prepare pumpkin: Wash, dry, and oil pumpkin. Pierce into center 3 to 4 times with skewer or sharp knife.

Conventional Oven: Place in cake pan. Add ¼ c. (60 mL) water to bottom of pan. Tent with aluminum foil. Bake at 350° F (175° C) for 1½ hours or until tender. Cut off top third of pumpkin. Spoon out seeds; discard. Spoon out pulp, leaving enough around edges to make a solid shell. Whip the pulp with butter, honey, salt, cinnamon, and nutmeg. Return to shell. Garnish with pineapple chunks.

Microwave Oven: Wrap prepared pumpkin in plastic wrap or waxed paper. Cook on "High" for 12 to 15 minutes or until tender. Continue as for conventional oven.

Yield: 5 to 6 servings

Herb Cornish Game Hen

half	hen per person	half
1 c.	pure vegetable oil	250 mL
3 T.	parsley (chopped)	45 mL
2 t.	salt	10 mL
½ t.	marjoram	2 mL
½ t.	paprika	2 mL
½ t.	onion (minced)	2 mL
½ t.	thyme	2 mL
¼ t.	pepper	1 mL
¼ t.	tarragon	1 mL

Place hen halves in shallow pan. Combine vegetable oil and seasonings; pour over hens. Cover and allow to marinate at least 2 hours, turning occasionally. Drain off marinade and reserve. Place hens skin-side-down on greased cookie sheet. Broil 5 in. (12.5 cm) from heat for about 20 to 25 minutes. Turn and baste every 5 minutes with marinade.

Crown Roast of Pork

6-lb.	pork crown roast	3-kg
1 T.	salt	15 mL
½ t.	sage	2 mL
¼ t.	pepper	1 mL
dash	nutmeg	dash
	favorite stuffing	

Place crown roast in center of shallow roasting pan. Wrap bone ends with aluminum foil. Combine salt, sage, pepper, and nutmeg; sprinkle over roast. Bake at 350° F (175° C) for 1½ hours. Fill center with favorite stuffing. Return to oven. Bake 1 hour more or until golden brown. Slide carefully onto heated serving plate.

Yield: 8 to 10 servings

Canard à la Pamplemousse

5-lb.	duck	2-kg
	salt	
1	grapefruit	1
3 T.	sugar	45 mL
2 c.	Beef Stock (p. 37)	500 mL
1 T.	cornstarch	15 mL
	salt and pepper to taste	

Wash duck thoroughly. Prick skin all over with sharp fork. Salt cavity. Squeeze juice from grapefruit; reserve juice. Remove membranes from grapefruit halves and discard. Cut grapefruit halves into pieces. Stuff into duck cavity. Place duck breast-side-up on rack in shallow pan. Bake at 375° F (190° C) for 2 to 2½ hours or until leg moves easily. For pamplemousse glaze, combine reserved grapefruit juice, the sugar, Beef Stock and cornstarch in saucepan. Cook over low heat until slightly thickened. Add salt and pepper to taste. During the final 20 minutes of cooking, baste duck every 5 minutes with glaze. Serve remaining glaze in sauceboat.

Yield: 1 duck or 4–5 servings

Potato Nests

2 c.	potatoes (mashed)	500 mL
1	egg (separated)	1
1 t.	onion (grated)	5 mL
	favorite vegetable	
1 c.	white Cheddar cheese (shredded)	250 mL

Mix potatoes, egg yolk, and onion. Pile into 4 or 5 mounds on greased cookie sheet. With the back of a spoon, form into nests. Beat egg white until frothy; brush over potato nests. Fill with favorite vegetable. Sprinkle with cheese. Bake at 400° F (200° C) for 30 minutes or until lightly browned.

Yield: 4 to 5 servings

Pumpkin Bread

3½ c.	all-purpose flour	875 mL
2 c.	sugar	500 mL
1½ t.	salt	7 mL
1 t.	cinnamon	5 mL
1 t.	nutmeg	5 mL
2 t.	baking soda	10 mL
1 c.	shortening (melted)	250 mL
⅔ c.	water	160 mL
3	eggs	3
2 c.	pumpkin purée	500 mL

Combine dry ingredients in large mixing bowl. Add melted shortening, water, eggs, and pumpkin purée. Beat until smooth. Pour into two well-greased and floured 9 × 5-in. (23 × 13-cm) loaf pans. Bake at 350° F (175° C) for 1 hour or until toothpick inserted in center comes out clean. Cool slightly. Turn out onto racks.

Microwave: Cook on Low for 20 minutes; increase to High for 5 to 6 minutes or until toothpick inserted in center comes out clean. Turn dish a half turn every 5 minutes. Allow to rest 2 to 3 minutes. Turn out onto rack.

Yield: 2 loaves

Gingerbread

½ c.	sweet butter	125 mL
½ c.	sugar	125 mL
1	egg	1
2½ c.	all-purpose flour (sifted)	625 mL
2 t.	baking soda	10 mL
1 t.	cinnamon	5 mL
1 t.	ginger	5 mL
½ t.	salt	2 mL
1 c.	unsulphured molasses	250 mL
1 c.	water (hot)	250 mL

Cream together butter and sugar; add egg. Whip to blend. Combine flour, baking soda, spices, and salt; sift to blend. Stir molasses into hot water to blend. Add flour mixture and molasses mixture alternately to creamed mixture. Beat well after each addition. Pour into 9 × 13-in. (23 × 33-cm) greased pan. Bake at 350° F (175° C) for 45 minutes or until done.

Microwave: Pour into two 8-in. (20-cm) round dishes. Cook on Low 7 to 8 minutes, then on High for 4 to 5 minutes or until toothpick inserted in center comes out clean. Turn dish every 3 minutes. Allow to rest 2 to 3 minutes. Turn out onto rack.

Yield: 1 loaf

White Fruit Loaf

2 c.	all-purpose flour	500 mL
½ c.	pecans or walnuts (chopped)	125 mL
½ c.	unsweetened coconut (grated)	125 mL
½ c.	kumquats (seeded and chopped)	125 mL
½ c.	dates (chopped)	125 mL
½ t.	baking soda	2 mL
¼ t.	salt	1 mL
¼ c.	sweet butter	60 mL
2 T.	pure solid shortening	30 mL
1 c.	sugar	250 mL
1 t.	pure vanilla extract	5 mL
3	eggs	3

Combine ½ c. (125 mL) of the flour with nuts and fruits. Toss to coat. Place remaining 1½ c. (325 mL) flour, baking soda, and salt in flour sifter. Cream together butter and shortening; continue beating and gradually add sugar and vanilla extract. Beat until light and fluffy. Add eggs, one at a time. Beat to mix thoroughly. Sift in flour mixture. Beat to blend. Fold in fruit-nut mixture. Pour into 9 × 5-in. (23 × 13-cm) loaf pan, which has been lined with waxed paper and well greased. Bake at 350° F (175° C) for 60 minutes. Cool 15 minutes; remove to rack. Carefully remove waxed paper. Cool completely. This cake may be eaten immediately, frozen, or kept wrapped in aluminum foil in a cool place. For added flavor, sprinkle 2 T. (30 mL) grapefruit juice over cake every 10 days; repeat twice.

Yield: 1 fruit loaf

Cranberry Relish

2 c.	cranberries	500 mL
1 c.	crushed pineapple	250 mL
½ c.	nut pieces (pecans or walnuts)	125 mL
½ c.	sugar	125 mL

Put cranberries through food grinder or food processor. Add remaining ingredients. Store in refrigerator.

Yield: 3 c. (750 mL)

Candied Citron

½ c.	water	125 mL
½ c.	sugar	125 mL
	peel of grapefruit, lemon, or lime	

Combine water and sugar in saucepan. Stir to dissolve sugar; bring to boil. Boil 5 minutes; add citrus peel. Boil 10 minutes. Remove citrus from syrup. Dry. Store in airtight container or freeze. May be used for flavorings or decorations.

Yield: Depends on how much rind you add

Pulling Taffy

2 c.	sugar	500 mL
1½ c.	water	325 mL
1 c.	unsulphured molasses	250 mL
½ c.	sweet butter	125 mL
¼ c.	light corn syrup	60 mL

Combine all ingredients in saucepan. Cook and stir over low heat until sugar dissolves. Increase heat and bring just to boil. Boil to hard ball stage (250° F; 120° C). Pour onto greased cookie sheet or pan. Grease hands; pull taffy until light in color. Cut or shape into desired size.

Yield: 1½ lb. (750 g)

Steamed Mock Plum Pudding

1 c.	carrots (grated)	250 mL
1 c.	dates (chopped)	250 mL
1 c.	pecans (broken)	250 mL
2 t.	lemon peel (grated)	10 mL
2 t.	all-purpose flour	10 mL
1½ t.	baking powder	7 mL
½ t. each	cinnamon, nutmeg, salt	2 mL each
½ c.	sweet butter	125 mL
¾ c.	brown sugar (packed)	190 mL
1	egg	1
	optional: English Hard Sauce (p. 89)	

Combine carrots, dates, pecans, lemon peel, flour, baking powder, and seasonings in mixing bowl. Toss to completely coat. Cream together butter and brown sugar; add egg. Beat well. Fold into carrot mixture. Pour into greased mold; cover. Steam in Dutch oven 2 hours or until set. Unmold. If desired, serve with English Hard Sauce.

Yield: 8 to 10 servings

Citron Cookies

⅔ c.	pure solid shortening	190 mL
1 c.	sugar	250 mL
2	eggs	2
½ t.	salt	2 mL
½ t.	baking soda	2 mL
1 T.	lime rind (grated)	15 mL
½ t.	lime juice	125 mL
2¼ c.	flour	560 mL
	optional: Doughnut Glaze (p. 122)	

Cream together shortening and sugar. Add eggs, one at a time, and beat well. Add salt and baking soda. Add lime juice and rind and flour alternately to creamed mixture. Drop by spoonfuls onto greased cookie sheets. Bake at 375° F (190° C) for 10 minutes. If desired, glaze cooled cookies with Vanilla Glaze.

Yield: 5 to 6 dozen cookies

Dabbles and Doodles

1 c.	pure solid shortening	250 mL
1½ c.	sugar	375 mL
2	eggs	2
2¾ c.	all-purpose flour	690 mL
2 t.	cream of tartar	10 mL
1 t.	baking soda	5 mL
¼ t.	salt	1 mL
	assortment of nuts (not almonds)	
	dates	
	coconut pieces	
1 t.	cinnamon	5 mL
2 t.	sugar	10 mL

Cream together shortening and 1½ c. (375 mL) sugar; add eggs. Stir in flour, cream of tartar, baking soda, and salt. Surround nut, date, or coconut piece with dough, or roll dough into ball the size of a walnut. Roll cookie in cinnamon-sugar mixture. Place 2 in. (5 cm) apart on ungreased cookie sheet. Bake at 350° F (175° C) for 10 to 12 minutes. Cool on cooling racks.

Yield: 6 to 7 dozen cookies

Fruit Bars

⅔ c.	pure solid shortening	160 mL
½ c.	sugar	125 mL
2	eggs (separated)	2
1 T.	pure vanilla extract	15 mL
1¾ c.	all-purpose flour	440 mL
2 t.	baking powder	10 mL
1 t.	salt	5 mL
1 c.	milk	250 mL
½ c.	pure coconut (shredded)	125 mL
½ c.	dates (floured and cut up)	125 mL
¼ c.	Candied Citron, cut up (p. 178)	60 mL
¼ c.	pecans (chopped)	60 mL

Cream together shortening, sugar, egg yolks, and vanilla extract until light and fluffy. Blend flour, baking powder, and salt alternately with milk into creamed mixture. Stir in coconut, dates, Candied Citron, and pecans. Beat egg whites until very stiff. Fold into cookie dough. Spread into well-greased 14 × 10-in. (35 × 25-cm) cookie sheet. Bake at 375° F (190° C) for 35 to 40 minutes or until toothpick inserted in center comes out clean. Cool completely. Cut into 2 × 1-in. (5 × 2.5-cm) bars.

Yield: 35 bars

Children's Christmas Cookies

2	eggs	2
2	egg yolks	2
1 c.	sugar	250 mL
1½ t.	pure vanilla extract	7 mL
1½ c.	all-purpose flour	375 mL
¾ c.	cornstarch	190 mL
	Candied Citron (p. 178)	

Beat eggs, egg yolks, and sugar until light and lemon-colored; add vanilla extract. Sift together flour and cornstarch. Stir into egg mixture. Drop dough by spoonfuls onto greased cookie sheets. Top with small piece of Candied Citron. Bake at 350° F (175° C) for 8 to 10 minutes or until lightly browned. Cool on racks.

Yield: 5 to 5½ dozen cookies

PRODUCT INFORMATION

Product Information

This is a partial list of food products which meet the standards of the hyperactive diet. This list eliminates those products which contain artificial food coloring, artificial flavoring, BHT, and BHA. It DOES NOT eliminate fruits and vegetables with natural salicylates. Because formulas are sometimes changed by food manufacturers, it is wise to check the labels before using any product.

BEST FOODS, CPC INTERNATIONAL
        Argo/Kingsford/Duryea's Cornstarch
        Skippy Peanut Butter
        Karo Light Corn Syrup
        Oats (all kinds)
        Mazola Corn Oil
CARNATION COMPANY
        Carnation: Evaporated Milks (whole, lowfat, and
                    skim)
                 Instant Nonfat Dry Milk
                 Instant Malted Milk (natural, not choco-
                    late)
        Contadina: Tomato Paste
                 Tomato Heavy Puree
                 Tomato Sauce
                 Pizza Sauce
                 Round Tomatoes
                 Italian-Style Tomatoes
                 Stewed Tomatoes
                 Sliced Baby Tomatoes
                 Seasoned Bread Crumbs
                 Meat Loaf Mix

Albers: White Cornmeal
Yellow Cornmeal
Quick Grits

DANNON LOWFAT YOGURT
All flavors

DEL MONTE
Juices: Grapefruit (plain)
Orange
Unsweetened Pineapple
Prune
Tomato
Apricot Nectar
Pear Nectar
Seafoods: All kinds
Pickles: All pickles and pickle products

ESTEE CORPORATION
Joan's Natural Milk Bar
Joan's Natural Peanut Butter Carob Bar
Joan's Natural Honey Sesame Bar
Joan's Natural Fruit and Nut Bar
Sugar-Free Esteemints (peppermints)
Sugar-Free Esteemints (assorted mints)

GENERAL FOODS
Baker's German Sweet Chocolate
Baker's Unsweetened Chocolate
Brim Decaffeinated Coffee
Calumet Baking Powder
C. W. Post Hearty Granola Cereal
C. W. Post Hearty Granola Cereal with Raisins
Instant Postum Cereal Beverage (not coffee flavor)
Maxim 100% Freeze-Dried Coffee
Maxwell House Coffee
Post Frosted Rice Krinkles Cereal
Post Raisin Bran
Post Super Sugar Crisp Sweetened Wheat Puffs
Sanka Brand 97% Caffeine-Free Coffee
Yuban Coffee
Bird's Eye Regular or Plain Frozen Vegetables (with the
exception of the potato products)

INTERNATIONAL MULTIFOODS
Kretschmer Wheat Germ

LA CHOY

The major portion of this line does not contain artificial colors, flavors, BHT, or BHA. **The following are exceptions:**

La Choy Product	Artificial Color	Artificial Flavor	BHT and/or BHA
Canned Chicken Chow Mein (16-oz. size only, not bi-pack)	no	no	yes
Canned Meatless Chow Mein (16-oz. size only, not bi-pack)	no	no	yes
Canned Shrimp Chow Mein (including bi-pack)	no	no	yes
Fortune Cookies	no	no	yes
Frozen Szechwan Dinners	yes	yes	no
Frozen Chinese Vegetables	no	yes	no
Glass Pack Hot Mustard	no	yes	yes
Glass Pack Plum Sauce	no	no	yes
Glass Pack Sweet and Sour Sauce	no	yes	yes
Ramen Noodles (beef, chicken, Oriental)	no	no	yes

LORANN OILS
Natural Anise Oil
Natural Clove Oil
Natural Lemon Oil
Natural Lime Oil
Natural Orange Oil
Natural Spearmint Oil

MORTON SALT
Morton Plain Table Salt
Morton Iodized Table Salt

ORE-IDA FOOD, INC.
Golden Crinkle French-Fried Potatoes
Golden Fries
Golden Shoestrings
Dixie Crinkles

ORE-IDA FOOD, INC. (cont'd)

> Country-Style Dinner Fries
> Cottage Fries
> Heinz Self-Sizzling Deep Fries (shoestrings, crinkle cut, regular cut)
> Tater Tots
> Shredded Hash Browns
> Southern-Style Hash Browns
> Small White Peeled Potatoes
> O'Brien Potatoes
> Stew Vegetables
> Frozen Sweet Corn (cob or cut)

PEPPERIDGE FARM, INC.

> All products

PILLSBURY COMPANY

> Flour (all varieties)
> Enriched Farina
> Pancakes (all flavors)
> Sweeteners (Sprinkle Sweet)
> 1869 Brand Baking Powder Heat 'n Eat Biscuits
> 1869 Brand Buttermilk Heat 'n Eat Biscuits
> Microwave Popcorn

RALSTON PURINA COMPANY

> Ralston Quick Oats
> Ralston, Dixie Bell or Tea Flake Snackers
> Ralston or Dixie Bell Oyster Crackers
> Ralston Saltines
> Natural RyKrisp
> Chicken of the Sea Tuna (canned)

SARA LEE

> Apple Pie
> Dutch Apple Pie
> Blueberry Pie
> Cherry Pie
> Peach Pie
> Pumpkin Pie
> French Cream Cheese Cake
> Cherry Cream Cheese Cake
> Strawberry Cream Cheese Cake
> Strawberry French Cream Cheese Cake

SARA LEE (cont'd)
>Chocolate Bavarian Cream Cheese Cake
>Pound Cake
>Chocolate Pound Cake
>Chocolate Swirl Pound Cake
>Banana Nut Pound Cake
>Raisin Pound Cake
>Homestyle Pound Cake

STOKELEY-VAN CAMP, INC.
>All canned and frozen fruits and vegetables

WESTERN DRESSINGS, INC.
>Coleslaw
>Creamy Italian
>Mayonnaise
>Shrimp Sauce
>Sweet 'n Sour
>Western

APPENDIX

BIBLIOGRAPHY
of books and pamphlets available from ACLD

Can Your Child Read, Is He Hyperactive?, by W. Crook, MD
Coping with the Hyperactive, by C. Cima
Eliminating the Additives, by John Wacker
Food Dyes and Hyperkinetic Children, by Hawley and Buckley
The Hyperactive Child, by B. Black
The Hyperactive Child, by Domeena Renshaw, MD
The Hyperactive Child (A Handbook for Parents), by Paul Wender, MD
Hyperactive Children (Diagnosis and Management), by Daniel Safer and Richard Allen
Hyperactivity, by M. Kinsbourne and Swanson
Hyperkinesis and Learning Disorders as Symptoms of Medical Problems, by S. Walker III
The Nutritional Aspects of Learning Disorders, by M. Hoffman, MD
The Overactive Child (reprint), by L. Eisenbert
A Parent's Guide to Hyperactivity in Children, by K. Minde, MD
Treatment of the Hyperactive Child, by R. Wunderlich
When Your Child Is Hyperactive, by Kenneth Heiting
Why Your Child Is Hyperactive, by Ben Feingold, MD

ORGANIZATIONS

Association for Advancement of Behavior Therapy
420 Lexington Ave., New York, New York 10017

Association for Children and Adults with Learning Disabilities
4156 Library Road, Pittsburgh, Pennsylvania 15234

Council for Children with Behavioral Disorders
1920 Association Drive, Reston, Virginia 22091

Foundation for Children with Learning Disabilities
99 Park Ave., New York, New York 10016

Index

191

About the Author

Mary Jane Finsand's lifelong interest in medical diets was chan-
neled into writing the best selling *The Complete Diabetic Cookbook*
(Sterling Publishing Company) after her neighbor's son was diagnosed as a diabetic. The success of that book prompted the chemist-
turned-nutritionist to compile this volume of varied, nutritious, and
enjoyable meals for hyperactive children and their families, basing
her recipes on the well-known Feingold diet plan.

Mary Jane is active in a number of children's and young adults'
groups. She has acted as editor on Metric Project Activity Books and
as consultant on Science Activity Books at the University of Northern
Iowa. Mary Jane lives in Cedar Falls, Iowa with her husband, D.
Louis Finsand. They have four children.